Merchant Writers

Merchant Writers

of the

Italian Renaissance

edited by

Vittore Branca

translated from the Italian

by

Murtha Baca

MARSILIO
PUBLISHERS
NEW YORK

Originally published as *Mercanti Scrittori*
© 1986 Rusconi

Copyright © 1999 Marsilio Publishers
Marsilio Publishers
P.O. Box 1039
Cooper Station
New York, NY 10003
www.marsiliopublishers.com

All Rights Reserved
Printed in the United States of America

LOC 92-62368

Library of Congress Cataloging-in-Publication Data

Mercanti scrittori.   English
    Merchant Writers of the Italian Renaissance / edited by Vittore Branca ; translated from the Italian by Murtha Baca.
      p. 218   cm. 13.97 x 21.59
    Includes bibliographical references.
    ISBN 1-56886-058-7 (pbk.)
    1. Florence (Italy)—Social life and customs.   2. Commerce––History—Medieval, 500–1500.   3. Merchants—Italy—Florence––Biography.   4. Florence (Italy)—Commerce—History.   5. Florence (Italy)—Biography.   I. Branca, Vittore.   2. Baca, Murtha.
    DG735.6.M4713   1999
    945' .51—dc21   99-39085
                                                CIP

Marsilio Publishers' books are available from
Consortium Book Sales & Distribution
800-283-3572

Contents

Introduction	vii
Bibliographic Note	li
Giovanni Boccaccio:	
Decameron Day II, Tale 5	3
Decameron Day II, Tale 9	17
from *Letter to Francesco Nelli*	31
Domenico Lenzi il Biadaiolo, from *Mirror of Humanity*	37
Paolo da Certaldo, from *Book of Good Practices*	45
Giovanni di Pagolo Morelli, from his *Ricordi*	51
Bonaccorso Pitti, from his *Ricordi*	89
Donato Velluti, from his *Ricordi*	111
Goro Dati, from his *Secret Book*	125
Francesco Datini, from his *Last Will and Testament*	133
Lapo Niccolini de' Sirigatti, from *Book of Family Affairs*	139
Bernardo Machiavelli, from his *Ricordi*	143
Lorenzo de' Medici, *A Brief Account*	153
Niccolò Machiavelli, *Letter to Francesco Vettori*	159

Introduction

In the *Decameron*, Boccaccio recounted the epic of the Italian merchants of the thirteenth and fourteenth centuries in Europe, and even on the African and Asian shores of the Mediterranean.[1]

In the thriving civilization of the late Middle Ages in Italy, Florence was one of the main centers of the new power that was infringing on the power of the military and the power of the Church, and was a prime mover of the "economic revolution" (as Robert S. Lopez defined it) that characterized the age straddling the thirteenth and fourteenth centuries.[2] Economic power conditioned both the political and military power of kings and lords and the religious power of popes and bishops. Merchants and bankers could "make and break" kings, as one of them, Nicola Acciaiuoli (who had done so with the King of Naples), said. They could start and stop wars at the drop of a hat (as Bardi and Peruzzi did with France and England); they could get popes elected, have prelates and lords excommunicated (as Acciaiuoli and Frescobaldi did). Merchants had become the "fifth element" of the universe, along with air, water, earth, and fire. They were the "pillars of

---

1. See Bibliographic Note at end of this essay on my previously published studies of Boccaccio and the narrative tradition in Medieval and Renaissance Italy.

2. In *The Birth of Europe*; see Bibliographic Note.

Christianity" — that is, of civilization — as the famous historian of the time, Giovanni Villani, characterized them. Florence was the great center of banking and commerce in continental Europe and, through the Angevins in Naples, the Byzantine world as well; it dominated the new, the first true economic-commercial organization, based on the invention of double-entry accounting, on the letter of exchange that made it possible to move millions beyond any frontier, and on the stability and internationality of money (during the late Middle Ages, the Florentine florin played the same role that the dollar does today).

Boccaccio himself had gone back and forth between France and Italy, Greece and Asia Minor between about 1330 and 1340, when he was working for the powerful Bardi trading company of Angevin Naples. Thus he had been in a position to appreciate the "totally material" writing of annotations, diaries, and first-hand accounts by those busy men of action who worked for the banking-commercial-industrial "companies." Boccaccio made these often exceptional people the protagonists — be they heroes or victims — of several tales in his masterwork, the *Decameron*. He captured the uninhibited, bold, adventurous character of these men who travelled throughout Europe and from one side of the Mediterranean to the other. He portrayed their commitment, their culture, and their pioneering spirit, indirectly giving his seal of approval to their writings, in which those talents and that adventurous, exciting life were reflected.[3]

It was no accident that the earliest merchants to take up the pen were two men who worked in the circle of the Boccaccio family; in fact, one of them, Paolo da Certaldo, was from Boccaccio's home town. And it is no coincidence that in the wake of certain pages by Boccaccio, the first-hand accounts of Italian merchants in later years took the form of a fascinating, original literature that characterized the most advanced civilization of the

---

3. I will not dwell on Boccaccio here, since my writings on the *Decameron* are well known, also in the English translation of my book *Boccaccio: The Man and His Works*; see pp. 276–307, "The Mercantile Epic," where I examine the tales with merchant protagonists, also alluding to the works of the merchant writers.

Introduction

city-states of the late Middle Ages and High Renaissance, from Boccaccio to Machiavelli, Guicciardini, and Cellini all the way to the diarists of the sixteenth and seventeenth centuries. This was a genre of writing that flourished in hundreds of examples and different experiences, a genre that is now studied side by side with the Petrarchan genre of lyric poetry, the narrative genre established by Boccaccio, and the romantic-chivalric genre, as one of the most typical of Italian society and culture between the fourteenth and seventeenth centuries (and as the richest source of private diaries before the French diarists of the late Renaissance onward).

This was a genre that might proudly proclaim the fourteenth-century motto: "No enterprise, no matter how small, can begin or end without these three things: power, knowledge, and love."[4] And the revival of interest in it seems in some way natural in our own times — an interest in writers not of words but of facts and concrete realities, in writings that are not literary, but rather colloquial, personal accounts of the everyday realities and problems of ordinary men concerned with goods and money, home and family, private and public affairs; men with the urge to possess and dominate and the awareness of how fleeting it all is, man's pride and his inadequacies, his aggressive materialism and his insuppressible need for God.

The middle-class merchants of the late Middle Ages and early Renaissance felt and lived and took for granted these eternal realities of man and existence — not in an intellectual or literary way, but in the most ordinary way, in their own everyday activities. They recorded their memoirs in the direct, concrete tone of entrepreneurs who left room for emotions, imagination, and fantasy alongside accounts and calculations. They wrote about things and events and people involved in production; they were writers like Edison, Ford, Krupp, Gualino, Pirelli, Mattioli, and Rusca from the recent past, or Iacocca, Agnelli, Floriani, Travaglia, Renault, and Pompidou today. They were experiencing those realities at a time — like ours — when the ideals and powers and institutions

---

4. See Sapori, *Studi di storia economica*, I, p. 533.

Introduction

(Church and Empire) that had ruled society for centuries were in a state of crisis, and the ones that would dominate society in the centuries to come (supra-national economic institutions, large nations and their national agendas) were coming into being.

Most of these merchants were writing in the tempestuous atmosphere of the decline of the Florentine city-state and its guilds: the time between the brief, naive, populistic Ciompi rebellion in 1378 and the signory of the by then ruling Florentine family, the Medici, who had already been cunningly working behind the scenes in the person of Salvestro de' Medici at the time of the Ciompi uprising. This was also the time of Florence's most intense, dogged, aggressive campaign for supremacy not only in Tuscany, but in all of Italy.

Corresponding to the turbulently evolving political situation, on the economic level there was the first ascendancy of Florence during the thirteenth century (the florin was first coined in 1253) and the beginning of the fourteenth century, and then the economic depression during the mid-fourteenth century, with the dramatic failures of the houses of Bardi and Peruzzi and the devaluation of the florin, followed finally by the economic recovery of the late fourteenth century, which continued throughout the fifteenth. This was an economic-mercantile revolution, or rather an evolution less turbulent than the political upheaval but no less profound and decisive — and it had already been perspicaciously envisioned and foretold by Boccaccio in the mercantile epic of the *Decameron*.

A transformation of Florentine economic and social life took place starting at the time of the greatest European and Mediterranean expansion under the regime of the guilds and "companies" (there were about 200 guilds in Florence in the early fourteenth century), at the time of the most cautious albeit fortunate capitalistic organization, after the depression mentioned above, under the oligarchic domination of the wealthy and according to the directives, no longer of the guilds, but of the banks and "holding companies," which had their ultimate example in the Medici. The pioneering spirit of the adventurous merchants who had set out to conquer the Occident and the Orient, the discovery of

Introduction

new lands (Boccaccio himself recounted the discovery of the Canary Islands) out of a thirst for wealth and power but with a spirit of adventure and of human generosity as well, came to be supplanted by a systematic, cautious exploitation of those conquests through the accumulation of wealth. The powerful, explosive, expansive age of the Wool Guild, the Exchange, and the "companies" — the age of the Mozzi, the Frescobaldi, the Bardi, the Peruzzi, and the Acciaiuoli dynasties — was succeeded by the age of the highly calculating, almost inordinate cautiousness of the Datini, Albizzi, Strozzi, Ricasoli, Capponi, Pitti, Niccolini, Alberti, and Medici families. These families were also concerned about controlling the political situation in order to profit from the *monti* (public funds), to be able to obtain reductions on taxes and forced loans, to establish international relationships of privilege, or even to set up monopolies via official missions and with the backing of popes and kings.

The audacious, mad dash for wealth, the building of capital via the most open, ruthless economic cycle (from usury to exploitative production to dumping), the conquest of the European and Mediterranean markets even at the cost of violence, gave way to a cautious, deliberate quest for solid property investments, farming, or easy shortcuts to wealth (gambling, diplomatic posts as a source of "insider trading," manipulation of currency values). The motto of these new merchants seems to have been the one we find in Morelli: "Don't do too much; it's better to play it safe." Little by little, the various "companies" that had operated as far away as the distant lands of the Orient were replaced by banks that concentrated their operations on money — often public monies — in Florence, Italy, and Western Europe. In spite of a pathetic effort to create a "broad florin" in 1422, the Florentine florin, the true "dollar" of the late Middle Ages, was losing to the Venetian ducat its position as the prevailing currency of Europe and the Mediterranean.

The finest books of memoirs, the richest in humanity and narrative spirit, from those of Velluti, Morelli, and Pitti to those of Bernardo Machiavelli, reflect this tempestuous political and social background, rhetorically dominated by the values and myths (justice, peace, civic unity) of the *libertas* of the Florentine city-state. But later these myths came to be disturbed by blinding flashes of light and sinister shadows, great nostalgia and anguished shudders, by intractable hatreds and ambitions run wild, by appalling greed and headstrong enthusiasm, leading up to Lorenzo de' Medici's humanistic myths of a Florentine primacy in Italy and Europe and the prophetic illusions and upheavals of Savonarola.[5]

These writings by merchants and traders had already begun to appear in Florence during the thirteenth century, in the margins of ledgers and account books, where they recorded the acquisition of lands or the leasing of farmland to sharecroppers (as in the diaries of the Guicciardini family). These notations were also family histories and *ricordanze* (that is, "things to be remembered").[6] The awareness of the natural convergence of economic prosperity, power, and the growing fortunes of the family was always the inspiration for these books, which were often written by several members of successive generations of a family: as with the Medici, from Foligno di Conte in 1360 to Lorenzo the Magnificent in 1472. They were usually called *ricordi* or *ricordanze* or "book of . . ." with the name of the writer or of the family.

Of course Florence also produced the kind of technical or geographic-statistical documentation or *pratiche* that were prevalent in other commercial centers and especially in Venice (the greatest example of which is Marco Polo's book); suffice it to recall the famous *pratica* of the mid-fourteenth century by Francesco Balducci Pegolotti.[7] But these seemingly "marginal" annotations in account books and ledgers almost always had the character of histories of family life (births, marriages, deaths, above all in their economic implications such as wills and divisions of property,

---

5. Girolamo Savonarola (1452–1498), the famous Dominican preacher and reformer whose zealous attempts to end corruption in Florence ended in his excommunication and execution as a heretic.
6. A word of Provençal origin first used in Italy in the late thirteenth century.
7. Francesco Balducci Pegolotti, *La pratica della mercatura*, edited by Allan Evans (Cambridge, MA, 1936).

dowries, contracts of sale, construction of houses, etc.); or even insights of a psychological nature about people with whom the merchants had business dealings, or with whom they corresponded, reflections on family, social, or political situations or on moral and religious implications, always noted in a strictly familiar tone, only for the eyes of other family members. In the early fourteenth century, as we shall see, Domenico Lenzi interspersed the monotonous columns of prices of cattle fodder at the Orsanmichele market with apocalyptic notes about famine and plague, which affected the oscillation of prices. These distant roots in personal account books reappear in the more elaborate writings of the fifteenth century, in the form of accounting abbreviations and in certain syntagmas or stylistic features, and even in the writers' habit of "making an accounting" of the most diverse operations or events.

While they were keeping track of their activities (loans, sales, purchases, letters of exchange, organization of craftsmen and workers), these "sons of Mercury" were also acquiring the habit of evaluating and characterizing times, things, and people. As Le Goff has shown, they replaced "the eternally renewed, perpetually unpredictable time of the natural world with a new, measurable time, focused and foreseeable."[8] And they established a literary tradition that traced its origins to the Roman *paterfamilias* but that also fused life and economic substance with life and family substance, like body and soul, like the circulation of the blood and spiritual activity. For these *mercatores*, the family was also the basic, fundamental cell of civic and political life, as in Morelli, and as theorized by the greatest humanists of those years, from Bruni ("nor can anything be perfect where the family does not exist," *Life of Dante*) to Ficino ("by leading your family you educate yourselves, you become experts, honored in the earthly republic and worthy of the heavenly," *Letter to Pelotto*). *Ragion di mercatura* (merchant interests) and *ragion di famiglia* (family interests) — the two dominant themes of the diaries of three centuries

---

8. *Tempo della Chiesa e tempo del mercante* (Turin, 1977), p. 13.

(albeit with notable variants, as we shall see) — clearly indicate this from the earliest examples of the genre.

The merchant writer was fully aware of the decisive value of his writings for both his economic activity and for the life of his family, which were inextricably linked. It was no coincidence that when a merchant wanted to have his portrait made, he usually had himself depicted in the act of writing. It was not by chance that Dino Compagni, in his survey of the various professions in the *Libro del pregio (Book of Merit)*, characterized the *pregio* (merit) of the merchant as "fine writing."

For financial and political reasons, these annotations and accounts, both mercantile and domestic, became even more necessary at the beginning of the fifteenth century. The merchant's activity had always been closely interwoven with his domestic life. But the growing impact of the public sphere on the private (and vice versa) during the early fifteenth century heightened the need for annotations that served both commercial and family interests. The establishment of the Florentine *catasto* or tax assessment[9] in 1427, the creation of the *Monte delle doti*[10] in 1425, and the increasing number of *prestanze*[11] due to continual wars, made it necessary to keep precise accounts of both financial and family matters. For that matter, at this same time the increasingly oligarchic structure of the Florentine government and the strengthening of the increasingly conservative Guelph party (1413) led men to reconstruct the stories of their families and to gather evidence and facts about their own past and present and those of their families.

For both economic activity and for family and public life, it was necessary to have all the elements and all the documents relating to a family's estate, past and present, clear and ready to hand. This was the only way to defend one's estate from the often aggressive intervention of the state and whoever dominated it at the

---

9. A sort of declaration of income with a list of the members of the household and their status.

10. The Dowry Bank, where money was deposited to create dowries for women of marriageable age. See note 7 to Bernardo Machiavelli's diary.

11. Forced loans made to the state by private citizens depending upon the size of their estate.

Introduction

moment. This also enabled men to aspire to become part of the oligarchy of the government, which was selected for primarily economic and commercial motives.

These conditions are reflected and even recommended in the insistent teaching, more practical than humanistic, that often led the diarists into long digressions, from the past of their parents to the future they hoped to build for their children and grandchildren.

Luca Pitti, who had been given his start on the commercial scene in 1423 by his father Bonaccorso, and who through luck, brains, and vigilance became the proverbial progenitor of the economic and political greatness of his family, decided in 1459 to lay the foundations of his splendid *palazzo* right in the area of Florence where his forefathers had lived — a *palazzo* that would perpetuate the Pitti name for centuries (Vasari wrote that "so much grandeur and magnificence have never been seen"). Luca went from playing a leading role in the oligarchy of the wealthy middle class under the Medici regime to having his praises sung by poets like Ugolino Verino and Benedetto Dei, to being considered one of the four most powerful citizens of Florence at the time of Cosimo de' Medici's death in 1464. He can be considered an emblematic figure in the sociopolitical situation reflected in the most characteristic writings of the merchants of the fourteenth and fifteenth centuries.

In the writings of the Florentine merchants, the preponderant convergence of commercial interests and family interests, over which the more ruthless state interests began to cast a shadow during the mid-fifteenth century, is depicted in various situations and in continual evolution, enlivened by the most diverse human temperaments. Underlying the most systematic and successful of these writings are usually moral reflection and debate; attention to and preoccupation with spiritual and domestic matters; and political and familial commitments and aspirations that also had a public, civic side to them. During the fifteenth century, family and political considerations came to be overshadowed by the personality of the individual writer; thus sometimes these writings constituted, at least in part, a kind of autobiography (for example in Bonaccorso Pitti's writings or in private diaries like those of Dati and Morelli, and later Lorenzo de' Medici), although they hardly lend themselves to any overly modern, intimistic affirmation or interpretation.

Throughout the fourteenth and during the early fifteenth centuries, Europe was still feeling the effects of the heated moral debates about the legality of the "lending" and "trading" that had begun to flourish during the second half of the thirteenth century. In response to the absolute, traditional opponents of exchanging currency, charging interest, and large profits (on the basis of the Old and New Testaments, but also Aristotle) — i.e., the very activities of the *mercatores* — there began to emerge new theologians and moralists (especially Franciscans) who were more indulgent toward banks and commerce, albeit within certain limits and under specific conditions. In any case, the first capitalistic organization subsequent to the almost exclusively rural feudal economy of the medieval courts was seen in a bad light and kept on the margins of Christian life. Commercial interests and authentic evangelical ethics seemed difficult to reconcile, as the Dominican friar Giordano da Pisa preached at the beginning of the fourteenth century.

For this reason, the writings of the merchants are pervaded by moral concerns, often expressed impersonally and in a categorical way through aphorisms and proverbs and reinforced by insistent moral and religious precepts. Two particularly exemplary, singularly effective writers — Domenico Lenzi and Paolo da Certaldo — stand out in this group.

Between 1320 and 1335, Domenico Lenzi, better known as *il Biadaiolo* (that is, a seller of *biade*, fodder), made long lists of grain prices on the Florentine market of Orsanmichele; completing them with lists for the period of 1309 to 1319, Lenzi collected them in a splendid illuminated manuscript (today designated as Tempi 3 in the Laurentian Library in Florence) under the highly religious, moralistic title of *Specchio umano* (Mirror of Humanity).[12] Lenzi unscrupulously profited from the ups

---

12. There is very little documentation on Lenzi, who put together his *Specchio* during the mid-fourteenth century, with a clearly literary and stylistic commitment and for a particular public. This was not a modestly secret, private family book.

and downs of the basic products necessary for man's very subsistence. But he also saw a providential occurrence in those fluctuations, as other merchants such as Giovanni Villani, Boccaccio, and Paolo da Certaldo were writing at the same time ("All the plagues and battles, ruins and floods . . . occur by the permission of divine justice, to punish men's sins" Villani, XI, 2; "the deadly plague . . . was sent upon mortals by the righteous ire of God to punish us for our evil deeds" *Decameron*, Introduction, 8; Paolo da Certaldo, precept 339). And this humble grain trader observed that divine design with moral and religious reflections, often in proverbs and verses written by himself and others, interspersed among the lists of prices and financial-agrarian annotations that occupy most of the manuscript (and which are extremely valuable documents for the history of economy, particularly agrarian economy, as Charles de la Roncière[13] and Giuliano Pinto[14] have thoroughly demonstrated).

Although Lenzi called himself a "coarse, ignorant writer," his work is a "merchant classic," as it has been repeatedly defined; he was also a lively, effective writer, guided by a keen awareness of the dignity of his work. He was a Christian who was well aware of the danger of considering gain to be a *raison d'être*, and of the need for human moderation. He was highly sensitive to the needs of "God's poor," and very conscious of the supernatural destiny of man.

This heartfelt awareness on the part of the writer, along with his commitment as a citizen — which at times reached the level of civic poetry — gave Lenzi's *Mirror* a place alongside Boccaccio's *Decameron* at the beginning of that evocative genre of mercantile narrative writing and in the history of private diaries and practical, social teachings that would lead to Francesco Guicciardini's melancholy, very human *Ricordi* in 1530.

Like no other writings of the time, the narratives of these merchant writers offered a tough, tragic chronicle of poverty and hunger, describing how the poor periodically went wild from

---

13. *Prix et salaires à Florence au XIVe siècle (1280–1380)* (Rome, 1982).
14. Giuliano Pinto, ed., *Il libro del biadaiolo: carestie e annona a Firenze dalla metà del '200 al 1348/di Domenico Lenzi* (Florence, 1978).

privation, from the desperate recourse to "plant roots and fruits of trees and meats that disgust not only the mouth, but the nose as well." In this sad, eternal epic of the struggle of the disinherited, crushed and swept along by civic or economic tragedies, Lenzi singles out desperate scenes of privation and violence with the pitiless figurative power of painters like Ambrogio Lorenzetti or Francesco Traini, using a turgid, vehement language reminiscent of the lower circles of Dante's *Inferno*.

Lenzi turned to Dante to seal his magnificent, moving description of the poor forced out of Siena in 1329 with a flourish of disdain (also ignited by Florence's inexorable hatred for her rival city-state, Siena). These are difficult, dramatic pages that in the first warmth of hope and charity focus on sweeping images of generosity reminiscent of Boccaccio's Nathan.[15] But then suddenly the rhythm changes, becoming fast and agitated: in the city of Siena's decision to drive out the poor ("all those to whom only God is a brother should be left to die of hunger"), in their desperate delusion of a return to the hospice that had once generously taken them in ("there arose infinite cries and sounds of hands striking, shouts and crying and people clawing their own faces"), in their anguished madness, which explodes in a storm of tumult followed by merciless repression:

> ... and the poor, running in infinite numbers toward the greatest palazzo ... cried out *Misericordia*, or *fire*, or *die* ... striking with stones and sticks ... driving [the armed men] back inside ... Several days later ... no fewer than 60 men were taken from their beds, and as many were slain with swords as were hung by the neck.

At the height of this tragedy of poverty and hunger, when "in a public council it was voted at last that the poor should be driven out of Siena and that no succor for the love of God was to be given them," Lenzi's antipathy erupts in the Dantesque cry:

Oh! Cruel earth, why did you not open up?[16]

---

15. *Decameron* Day X, tale 3.
16. *Inferno* XXXIII, 66.

Introduction

Perhaps while he was still alive and certainly right after his death, Dante was considered a teacher of both moral and religious faith as well as of noble poetry in the modest spiritual world of this "coarse, ignorant" grain merchant.

The class that was about to dominate late Gothic Florentine culture, and that would ultimately be painted in lively colors in Boccaccio's *Decameron*, could not fail to be part of the new public which, having first been won over to literature by Dante's *Divine Comedy*, developed tastes that would demand the art and literature of the second half of the fourteenth century. But already in these writings from the beginning of the century, the merchant class was asserting its heartfelt moral, social, and religious conscience and its talent for down-to-earth writing sustained by expressive power and some degree of literary and cultural experience.

These merchants, as Christian Bec has shown in his memorable studies of the fifteenth-century writers, were in fact quite sensitive to the moral message of the great writers, ancient and modern, from Cicero and Virgil and Seneca to Dante and Petrarch and Boccaccio; they were passionate readers and owners of those books.[17] As we shall see, they even took up the Ciceronian and Petrarchan *topos* of the free, fruitful "dialogue" between reader and exemplary texts, in a meditative, pedagogical sense. They not only had "ink-stained fingers" on account of the annotations necessitated by their profession; they also often had the ambition and the talent to write in order to communicate the human implications of their most routine activities, albeit only to those who were close to them. As Domenico De Robertis has shown in his history of fifteenth-century Italian literature, this was the sign "of a social and economic condition that had been achieved not by individuals but by an entire class of people: it was even a moral condition . . . a true literary *koiné* for the most part devoid of personal artistic aspirations, but that established a level of communication higher than that of spoken language."[18]

---

17. *Les marchands écrivains* and *Les livres des florentins*; see the Bibliographic Note at the end of this essay.

18. Domenico De Robertis, *Storia della letteratura italiana. Il Quattrocento* (Milan, 1966), p. 377.

Introduction

This moral and cultural situation of the mid-fourteenth century was amply confirmed by another grain merchant, Paolo da Certaldo, who had been designated to provide bread for the Florentine militias in 1362–1364.[19] Paolo, a compatriot and friend of Boccaccio (to whom he sold some land in 1360), the son of a prominent notary who worked on behalf of *mercatores*, had a certain degree of culture (as revealed by the literary echoes and allusions to Dante in his writings). He was a wise, active administrator, and above all a meditative moral observer in his *Book of Good Practices*, which is the masterwork of the moralistic, pedagogic merchant writings. Paolo's continual references to his own experiences and his disenchanted human realism seem in some way to prefigure the concrete, bitter style of Francesco Guicciardini. "It is better to act in vain than to do nothing in vain," concluded Paolo, as did Guicciardini: "The true praise is to be able to say: I did, I said."[20] And so on, with insistent Guicciardinian intuitions, continuously correcting and updating, mingling memories of family and society with mercantile admonitions and scenes and tales (precept 378) and amorous stories reminiscent of the *Decameron* (Boccaccio's tale of Andreuccio, II, 5, can be seen as an illustration of Paolo da Certaldo's precept 86).

Paolo's 388 precepts or proverbs have an entirely merchant-like character in the tone in which they are written or transcribed, in spite of the fact that almost half clearly derive from earlier sources of wisdom and that they are thrown together almost without rhyme or reason. In terms of the merchant's everyday life they offer, as Morpurgo noted, "a tiny, shimmering mirror which in rapid but clear flashes reflects many of the most ordinary and therefore rarely recorded customs [of the day]." When Paolo with

---

19. Very little is known about Paolo da Certaldo. His father was Messer Pace, a notary and man of the law, ambassador to Siena in 1318 and to Bologna in 1320, of the priors in 1323, of the Good Men in 1331 and 1336, standard-bearer of his guild in 1338, a man who could be trusted among merchants. Other than the two documents cited in the text we know nothing about Paolo except that he was unable to fulfill the terms of the contract for provisions for the Florentine troops and was fined, but obtained a pardon in 1370.

20. *Ricordi*, 129; Machiavelli echoes this sentiment in his own writings.

Introduction

his perspicacious eye observed the most ordinary aspects of his own everyday life, as Alfredo Schiaffini observed, "his writing is at its richest and most lively; he reveals his straightforward nature of a Florentine man of business, rich in experience, sharp and astute, ceremonious yet invincibly diffident, innately disposed to traffic in both goods and currency, and happy if he succeeds in saving his soul from eternal damnation as well as filling his purse with lovely clinking florins and acquiring more lands."[21]

In these writings, the family is closely linked to earning money and managing property:

> So that your family will be concerned with the good of your household, urge them not to come home empty handed; on the contrary, they should bring something home in their hands . . . because it is well to bring every good thing home (precept 89).

For Paolo, the only wealth that counted was wealth created by one's own toil; even inherited wealth was seen as uncertain and unpredictable (precepts 81, 352, and 385).

But moral and religious ends confront the demands of business and family:

> But take care that you do not deceive your own conscience (precept 250) . . . ill-gotten gains will not be forgiven until you return what you have taken (precept 128) . . . It will gain you nothing to do no evil, if you do not do good, for you will never go to heaven (precepts 32 and 388).

Thus a condemnation of usury and fraud is always present (e.g., in precepts 115, 128, and 321), even in the most venal of Paolo's precepts, even those that almost seem to condone deceit (precept 152) or unscrupulousness (precept 338). And the exhortation to charity and compassion is explained by the Catholic moral principle:

> If you do not have compassion for those who are in trouble, you shall not find mercy yourself; therefore always have compassion for your fellow-man, so that you can in good faith ask God for his compassion (precepts 33 and 388).

---

21. See Bibliographic Note.

Introduction

This is a kind of charity that derives in a certain sense from a mercantile, contractual view of things, from the notion of a pact with God (see also precepts 335 and 338). It is closely analogous to the famous bequests left "to Messire the Lord God" — that is, for alms — recorded in the account books of the Florentine guilds.[22] This was a practice that in the Gospels was always related to God, to a supernatural conception of life, impulses of sincere piety and religiosity (and this in spite of these merchants' open antipathy to the Pope — indeed their outright anti-clerical attitude), devoted to the point of daily visits to church and examinations of conscience. But while Paolo clung to the Christian vision of the Gospels as a renunciation of earthly things and as a preparation for heaven, he also remained faithful to the ethics and the practice of the merchants — to make the greatest profit possible — and to the economic and social success of the individual and of the family. As Christian Bec has observed, "Paolo da Certaldo was neither altogether forgetful of Christian morals, nor perfectly embued with the merchant ethic."[23] And yet Paolo's precepts often indicate a totally earthbound, middle-class ethic, in spite of frequent religious references, diligent thoughts of death and supernatural destiny, and faith in God and his providence (see for example precepts 335, 338, and 372).

This was a stretching, or rather a balancing act that went on continuously between the end of the fourteenth century and the beginning of the fifteenth century in several of these merchant writers, as in Dati, Lapo Mazzei, and in Datini, who was the most powerful, enterprising merchant of the time ("In the name of God and of gain," was his motto). In Mazzei and Datini, this provoked heated debates on the destiny of the soul, and, in Datini, the magnificent, memorable establishment of the Ceppo, a famous charitable institution that is still operating today, almost as a sort of "ransom" or redemption for an entire life immersed in trading and "gain." Along with the history of the family and the recording of his company's accounts and the sad recitals of financial

---

22. Sapori, *Studi*, II, pp. 839-ff.
23. In *Les marchands écrivains*.

Introduction

crashes, in his *Libro segreto* (Secret Book) Dati makes statements clearly analogous to those of Paolo da Certaldo, even to the point of verbal echoes ("In the name of God and the Virgin and of all the saints who grant us gain, with health of soul and body").[24] But when this balancing act was at its most difficult, it waved the banner of "tribulations of the soul" (perhaps also on account of commercial disasters), first in a moral crisis that led to a resolute examination of conscience, a personal "confession" with firm resolutions to reform ("since I realize that I have uselessly passed forty years since my birth with little obedience to God's commandments . . . I resolve . . ."). Then Paolo proposed subjugating the most ironclad motives of business and political success to the religious imperatives of piety and charity. But these are exceptions, perhaps caused also by Dati's entrance into public life and his serious financial difficulties, even the threat of bankruptcy (1404–1412). They are not unique, however, if we think of certain pages from the debate between Mazzei and Datini.[25] They were natural in a traditional temperament — a temperament that reflected the past more than the future, a temperament with inclinations to mysticism — like that of Dati, the brother of a

---

24. Gregorio or Goro di Stagio Dati (1362–1435), a silk trader, member of the Guild of Por Santa Maria, an active merchant, was Standard-bearer of Justice in 1428. He was unsuccessful in business. In 1348 he bought into a company for the first time, for 300 florins, and also traded with Spain. Perhaps on account of his unfortunate dealings with Spain, by 1412 he was on the verge of bankruptcy; he was saved by his brother Leonardo, a general in the Dominican order, and by Cosimo de' Medici.

25. The extremely interesting correspondence between Mazzei and Datini was published in two volumes, *Lettere di un notaro a un mercante del secolo XIV*, edited by C. Guasti, Florence, 1880. Guasti tells us that Mazzei (1347?–1412) was a prominent, cultured notary, a friend and counselor of Niccolò da Uzzano, Guido del Palagio, and other eminent Florentines; he was a colleague of Datini, whose will he drew up in 1410. On Datini (1333?–1410), one of the most famous merchants of the time, see the general studies of F. Melis, *Aspetti della vita economica medievale* (Florence, 1962), and the enjoyable biography by Iris Origo, *The Merchant of Prato: Francesco di Marco Datini 1135–1410* (Boston, 1982; first published in 1957). The correspondence reveals a continuous debate between the speculative, mystic notary and the merchant, a practical, down-to-earth man of business.

Introduction

Dominican vicar general who corresponded with Vallombrosan monks, the author of a *History of Florence* with a decidedly conservative, providential bent.

This balancing act between predominantly domestic economic and social imperatives and Christian ethics, between the various merchant traditions — civic, religious, and humanistic — is reflected in what is rightly considered to be the masterpiece of the merchant writers: Giovanni di Pagolo Morelli's *Ricordi*. Morelli interwove the history of his family and of his city with icastic portraits and narrative episodes as well as long moralistic and pedagogical digressions, financial precepts of a prevalently family nature, religious and emotional outpourings and self-analyses (of an almost psychological nature — Morelli had a complex about being an orphan), mystical reflections and visions, all pervaded by Morelli's deep-seated pessimism about man and by a wholehearted if tormented faith in God and his providence.[26]

Morelli evoked the wars for the rights of the Italian city-states against the feudal lords who still dominated the countryside in his frightening descriptions of the continuous struggles against "the tyrannical Ubaldini, robbers and destroyers of the Apennines and of the Mugello valley;" and in his recounting of the siege of Montaccianico, which he protracted like a sort of new *Iliad* ("the siege there went on for seventeen years" — instead of the four months it actually lasted). He transformed the siege into a sort of fabulous exploit of heroes on winged horses ("it was like doing battle with the stars"). He portrayed the fierce clashes between Florentine factions in similar dark, violent tones: "they fought from house to house with crossbows, and for this reason, many high, thick towers were built; you can still see many of them today inside the first circle [of the city]."

Even more immediate and direct was Morelli's awestruck evocation of the merchants who had made Florence into a world power through their group solidarity — men like Pagolo di Bartolomeo Morelli, who, "involved in dye trading for around

---

26. The *Ricordi* were written between 1393 and the early months of 1411; Morelli returned to them in 1421 only to record the death of his son Antoniotto.

Introduction

fifteen thousand florins . . . belonged to the Wool Workers' Guild and to the *Monte* and dealt in several thousand florins in direct exchanges and letters of exchange, French wools, and many other things") and always got out of scrapes with a profit to spare, even when his creditors were dropping like flies, and never ceased "going off to strange places to get merchandise, to sell it, and to keep everything going forward . . . at court and in Avignon he got his way, and not through the power of money, but by his own persuasive powers."[27]

Morelli's evocation of Florence in its early days and its first flourishing is liberally sprinkled with lively, robust portraits, which later evolved into profiles of wary, circumspect speculators or savers, especially in his insistent examples of diffident cautiousness. It seems that by this time the "strange lands" were too far away to be attractive; the adventurous wool trade and the daring art of money exchange had lost their fascination for Morelli. "It's better to play it safe" seems to have been the motto of this brand of calculating, pessimistic common sense, of this mode of behavior which, as in Paolo da Certaldo and Dati, has "the right way" as its supreme rule.

The uninhibited temerity of the creators of the great Florentine fortunes had given way to the guarded acquisitiveness of men who were looking for safe investments and were always worried about the state intervening in a fiscal or economic way. In Morelli, the oligarchy that during those years had an ironclad hold on the Florentine signory — and hence financial domination of the city — is depicted in its mercilessness in a series of rapid, impressionistic glimpses, lively portraits that are dramatic but not exhaustive. But first he paints a dark, deprecatory picture of the Ciompi rebellion, that brief revolt of the Florentine working classes:

> Then there rose up a wool worker named Michele di Lando, who remained Lord of Florence for three days; he sent out his own proclamations . . . During this time the *ciompi* never ceased to wreak havoc, to rob and to burn: Every street and doorway

---

27. Avignon was the seat of the Avignonese popes during the Western Schism (1378–1417).

was boarded up, and at night there were lamps burning in every window . . .[28]

After this sad glimpse of the poor masses run amok, but quickly squashed and scattered, comes the end of the tyrannical reign of Giorgio Scali:

> He was taken prisoner on his own doorstep, and brought before the Captain. Antonio di Bese [the *gonfaloniere* or chief magistrate of Florence] heard about this, and began to make a great fuss and to say that he had been betrayed . . . and that he was going to bring out the banner of Florence and didn't want a hair of Messer Giorgio's head to be touched. Filippo di Ser Giovanni had hidden the keys, and said: "Take it out, if you can." When Antonio saw the game was up and that all his grumbling was to no avail, he was forced against his will to agree with the others. Messer Giorgio's head was cut off, and Messer Tomaso di Marco fled, and Messer Donato de' Rico's head was cut off.[29]

Morelli's depictions of the continuous fighting and plotting among the Florentines are even more passionate and violent, shot through with dramatic tension. The sly shadow of Gian Galeazzo Visconti ("he dressed like a Franciscan monk, carried a rosary, and acted very benevolent") preyed on the fears of Morelli, who saw the Visconti dynasty of Milan closing in on his native city — until the triumphal march when the nightmare mysteriously disappeared.

Even more heated and implacable is the hatred for the Pisans that runs throughout Morelli's pages. For centuries, the Pisans were the thorn in the side of the Florentines' pride; the Florentines repeatedly defeated the Pisans, but never succeeded in dominating them. Morelli's hatred of the Pisans, like Pucci's in his *cantari*, swells to epic dimensions of contempt. Morelli gleefully dwelt on the humiliation of Florence's enemies after the victory of the Florentines over the Pisans in 1363:

> The Pisans were bound with their own ropes and loaded onto

---

28. The *ciompi* were the hired, propertyless workers in the wool industry.
29. The *gonfalone* was a banner or ensign, frequently composed of or ending in several tails or streamers suspended from a cross-bar, used by various Italian city-states.

fifty of their own carts; and in the first cart their eagle was hung, but not so that it would die, because its feet could reach the cart, and it was struggling violently. Their captain went in front, a prisoner, degraded . . . At the gate at San Frediano, through which the captain entered, there was a little live lion cub, and all the Pisan prisoners were forced to kiss its arse.[30]

Even during the twilight of the free Florentine city-state, Morelli remained strongly convinced of the providential function of the Florentine republic, which would surface during the tumult inspired by Savonarola, in the political mysticism of the *piagnoni*,[31] in the desperate heroism of the siege of Florence in 1530. "The holy, good City," and "the honor, state, greatness of the City" were always uppermost in Morelli's mind as a higher reality mandated by God, as a point of comparison and distinction between good and evil. But alongside the traditional, almost Dantesque nostalgia for "the good men of the Florence of old, Guelphs loyal to the city-state," Morelli sensed the rising tide against the tight-fisted oligarchy of the Ricci and the Albizzi (families that only Morelli among the historians of his time dared to criticize). In spite of his natural diffidence as a middle-class Guelph, Morelli was aware of the need to revamp the political character of Florence in a way that was more open to the common people.

In this solid faith, this love for the Florentine state that reached Manichean proportions, the state did not represent an absolute, beyond any moral or principle, as a hundred years later it would for Machiavelli represent the concrete realization, mandated by God, of a social and political order necessary for man to fully realize himself. As Hans Baron showed in his time,[32] and recently Leonida Pandimiglio has taken up, this was a continuation of the most authoritative Medieval, Dantesque line of thought, albeit filtered and interpreted through the sensibility of the early Florentine humanists — the ideal arc that inscribes very different

---

30. The *marzocco* or lion cub was a symbol of Florence, as the eagle was of Pisa.

31. The "lamenters," the nickname given to Savonarola's followers.

32. *The Crisis of the Early Italian Renaissance: Civic Humanism and Republican Liberty in an Age of Classicism and Tyranny* (Princeton, 1955).

writers, from a strict humanist like Poggio Bracciolini ("If human life were deprived of the fatherland, our virtue would undoubtedly be left frozen, isolated, sterile . . .") to a Christian Platonist like Matteo Palmieri ("no work among men can be more excellent than providing for the health of the fatherland and preserving the state . . .").

Palmieri, who of all the Florentine moralists had the most affinity to Morelli, seemed to be defining the core of Morelli's *Ricordi* when he wrote: "No other love touches us more than the love of our fatherland and of our own children." The great dominating passion of the cautious, diffident merchant Giovanni Morelli was the family in all its aspects.

The family was constantly at the center of Morelli's emotional, imaginative, and political life; it was the most consistent point of reference in his account of the history of Florence. It was the motive behind his most generous, human impulses and his most moving, limpid descriptions. It was the secret, supreme measure by which he judged, calculated, and acted. It was the dominating idea that somehow justified and redeemed even his base slynesses, his subtle moments of vulgarity, his completely utilitarian matrimonial strategies. If during the preceding era the Florentine signory had been recognized as a *ragion di mercatura*, and in the following era it became a *ragion di stato*, for Morelli we can speak of a *ragion di famiglia* — which could be more merciless and inhuman the more it was driven by family motives and the most generous of natural laws.

The power of Morelli's *ragion di famiglia* can be seen in the most sensitive, delicate component of his *Ricordi*: their linguistic fabric.[33] If this is the ultimate demonstration of the centrality of the family — descriptions, spiritual and economic reflections, pedagogical, moral, and health precepts (which recall Paolo da Certaldo), public and private memories — it all converges in function of and "for the health of our family . . . and for the honor and surpassing love of our own flesh and blood." The one time

---

33. See my *Con amore volere: narrar di mercatanti fra Boccaccio e Machiavelli* (Venice, 1996).

Introduction

that Morelli really let himself go was in his description of the Mugello[34] (where he was born), "the loveliest place in our whole countryside," painted with the freshness of a Fra Angelico or a Paolo Uccello, "out of love for our past," and with a significant convergence of beauty and utility. Morelli's most vivid portraits are of the "heroes of the family" — men and women (Calandro, Bartolomeo, Pagolo, Mea, Sandra) who, as Morelli puts forth in the first part of his *Ricordi*, founded or characterized the destiny of the Morelli family — a modest family from the Mugello that rose to wealth and great honors by hard work, honesty, and unshakable devotion to the "Catholic Guelf party." These are affectionately portrayed figures, with an eloquent immediacy, especially when they are captured in moments of domestic *pietas*. One example is Gualberto di Giovanni, who as a young man during the plague of 1374 took care of more than twenty relatives of his who had fled to Bologna. Morelli also presented these figures in scenes of domestic happiness, in courteous attitudes and gestures that were the natural reflection of their joyful inner civility. Thus we see Mea di Pagolo, luminously alive, like a figure in a painting by a late Gothic master.

Alongside Mea is a whole gracious series of serene, prudent women, "sweet in character" and "housewifely" — the foundation of their families' fortune and strength and of an intelligent, human approach to domestic economy. Morelli also sketched an amiable series of young boys and girls in all their vulnerable timidity.

The most intense, moving moment in Morelli's *Ricordi* occurs when he recounts the anguished moment of the death of Alberto, his first-born son: the painful memories of all the sweetest, most tender moments, even "when I could feel him with my hand, moving in his mother's belly, and awaited his birth with the greatest anticipation." Morelli initially gave himself over to the all-too-human abandon of an image that pursued him continuously. From this sorrowful, disconsolate tenderness arose Morelli's grand, almost epic evocation of his dead son, and his inconsolable

---

34. An area Southwest of Florence, between the Apennine ridge and the Arno Valley.

realization of the vanity of his own life: vain because he let the most intimate tendernesses, the most cherished values, the most basic affections slip through his fingers:

> The best news you ever had was when your wife had your first child, and this was turned into the greatest sorrow and the greatest torment you ever had. Your first child had to be a son, so that his death would really break your heart. You saw him intelligent and healthy, so when you lost him you would suffer more; you loved him and yet you never gave him any of your wealth. You didn't treat him like a son, but like a stranger; you never gave him a moment's rest; you never looked on him kindly; you never kissed him once; you worked him to death in your shop . . .

Against the backdrop of Morelli's regret for the joys he rejected and had lost forever, the diarist looks back in anguish at his own life, almost as a sort of "everyman" story with the added depth of a father's love discovered precisely at the moment when it has become futile.

One might almost say that this vision, or rather this moment of meditation in which human events are strongly associated with eternal values — often with devotional references to St. Catherine, the Blessed Dominici, and St. Antoninus, to whom Morelli was particularly devoted — brings to a close the diary that Morelli had written precisely to communicate to his family the meaning and the truth of life.

The "everyman story" that brings Morelli's *Ricordi* to an ideal conclusion would not be as effective and dramatic if the stage hadn't been set for it by his natural capacity for moralistic reflection. Such a perspective would be inconceivable in the lively, fascinating diaries of Donato Velluti and Bonaccorso Pitti, although their works, too, contain a wealth of human observation.

In Morelli, instead, accounts of family and civic life, private and public lessons learned, quick or studied portraits of people, descriptions of landscapes or events, are all enlivened and given greater depth by a constant moral pondering. Even in Morelli's presentation of historical events, which he usually narrated with great precision, we find him always striving to discover an element

Introduction

of providence and to relate the outcomes of individual actions to the moral commitment of those who carried them out.

It is upon this tireless quest for a moral interpretation of life's experiences at the core of Morelli's *Ricordi*, that his ample supply of precepts is naturally and coherently built — not as an episodic excursus or oratorical pause, but rather as an essential element of the architecture of the work.

Even classical culture is inscribed within the central motifs of Christian ethics in Morelli's work; because, as Bruni stated in a letter to Pope Eugenius IV, "the philosophy that deals with manners, the governance of states, and the best way to live one's life is almost equal in the pagan philosophers to our own."

For Morelli, as for Bruni and later for his friend Giovanni Dominici, the study of antiquity had an essentially moral value, constituting an awareness of man's dignity:

> ... when you come of age and your intellect begins to savor the reason for things and the sweetness of knowledge, you shall derive as much pleasure out of it, as much delight, as much consolation as you do out of anything in the world. You shall not prize so much wealth, children, status or any great or honorable preeminence, once you have knowledge and can repute yourself a man and not a beast.

He then adds, in a more realistic, practical tone, already prefiguring the final moment of pride and vain hope that springs from a bitter lack of faith reminiscent of Guicciardini ("How those who bring in the Romans at every word deceive themselves! There should be a whole city set aside just for them," otherwise "it would be like expecting an ass to run like a horse.").

> ... you can take as an example a valiant Roman or some other valorous man that you have studied. But it is not possible to imitate men like these as you can men whom you see with your own eyes, and especially in the things with which we have to deal, which are more material than those of the great events of Rome.

Thus for Morelli the eternal moral truths were already the precious patrimony of the ancients, before they were accommodated and affirmed with new strength within the Christian message.

Introduction

Consequently, for Morelli the study of the classics, both ancient and modern (up to Dante and Boccaccio, whom Morelli mentioned repeatedly) had a privileged place in everyday life, along with prayer, as a source of the truest wisdom and the deepest humanity.

For this Florentine merchant, study and meditation were not only a consolation and a comfort, but also — beyond the Ciceronian *topos* of man conversing with a book — rules of life, founts of action, as a hundred years later for Machiavelli they would be "that food which is mine alone, and for which I was born." But this solid middle-class merchant, more realistic than Machiavelli, placed the great texts of contemporary wisdom alongside "the ancient courts of ancient men." Above all, he valued direct, real-life experience, because, as Guicciardini would say, "It is a great mistake to speak of the things of the world indistinctly . . . discernment and restraint are not found written in books; they must be taught by discretion."

In that silent daily conversation with divine voices and the greatest human voices, felt as the expression of the Word of God, in that meditative space reserved every day for the peaceful pondering of one's own life experiences, lies the secret of the intensity of perspectives and nuances that adds greater depth to Morelli's accounts of domestic and historical events, spiritual and financial episodes, realistic portraits of men and things.

Various accounts dating from the time of Morelli to the beginning of the fifteenth century have a more personalized, more Machiavellian outlook.

In the diary he kept between 1367 and 1370, Donato Velluti[35] focused strictly on personal matters, above all the characters of individuals and their "virtues;" his goal was clearly that of glorifying

---

35. Donato Velluti (1313–1370), a judge, jurist, and merchant, was the son of Lamberto di Filippo Velluti. After holding various public offices, he was named Standard-bearer of Justice in 1370.

his own family. He too, at times, had conflicting moralistic preoccupations (he denounced usury, but admired it in one of his ancestors, and clearly for him love of the fatherland and the passion for business both sprang from family interests). Activities other than those of the merchant were viewed with diffidence by this judge who saw everything from the perspective of business.

But Velluti felicitously expressed family interests in a sort of "saga," especially in certain descriptions of his enterprising ancestors, unscrupulous relatives, and friends, both good and bad. These are often stylized portraits that take the form of quick sketches and impressions, richer in characteristic gestures than in inner life (such as those of Madonna Diana and Bonaccorso di Piero). Velluti's work took on a resolutely self-celebratory tone when he became more openly autobiographical in the last part of the book, although he repeatedly declared that what he was writing was not to praise himself, but out of love for his family.

Indeed, in the last portion of his account Velluti clearly intended to promote himself in the political arena; hence a great deal of space was given to the actions of the narrator himself, including swashbuckling adventures and escapades. Velluti showing himself in the act of carrying out public offices or missions, even in battles and episodes involving the emperor, had a certain exemplary significance, but also acted as a sort of "advertisement" for his family. As Bec has hypothesized, when his family's fortunes seemed to be coming to an end and could no longer aspire to political power, Velluti's reason for writing "to perpetuate the memory of the Velluti family" also seemed to dwindle away.

In 1379, shortly after the sad end of Velluti's story, Lapo Niccolini de' Sirigatti began to write his book "about the affairs of our family."[36] Much more than Velluti, Lapo became a rich, powerful representative of the Florentine oligarchy. A respected

---

36. Lapo di Giovanni Niccolini de' Sirigatti (1360?–1430), a prosperous merchant, had great success in the Wool Guild; he held numerous public offices and was Standard-bearer of Justice five times (in 1401, 1406, 1412, 1421, and 1425). He died on December 24, 1430 in the service of the Florentine state, as Vicegerent of the town of Vico Pisano.

member of the powerful Wool Guild, during the span of time when he was writing his book (1379–1427), Lapo constantly increased both his wealth and his political power. While obviously superior to Velluti in practical matters and success in life, Lapo was clearly Velluti's inferior as a writer. After the usual invocations, Lapo immediately began to boast about how old his family was; with their roots in Florence for at least seven generations, always living "in their houses in the street of the Palazzo of the Podestà," as he himself did; always victorious over the threatened loss or damage to their ancestral home. Investments and purchases of real estate generally have a consortial-familial motif in Lapo's writings: to maintain the authoritative presence of the Niccolini family in their original quarter of Florence, to enhance their credit and their good name with their real-estate holdings, also with an eye to obtaining public offices.

Bonaccorso Pitti must have been familiar with Velluti's book, which he certainly included among the "old writings of ours" that interested him so much; he was a relative of Velluti and a colleague of Niccolini, and, like Morelli, related by marriage to the Alberti and Acciaiuoli families.[37] He was a merchant and a politician, a skillful negotiator and ambassador, a good writer who turned out poetry that revealed an in-depth knowledge of Dante; he was well versed in late Gothic and early humanistic

---

37. Bonaccorso di Neri di Bonaccorso Pitti (1354–1432) came from a wealthy, solid family of merchants; he himself was a merchant and carried out numerous missions throughout Europe, was elected to several important offices and was Standard-bearer of Justice in 1417 and 1422. He was certainly the most active and adventurous of the Florentine diarists, and, along with Niccolini, the most prominent politically. Because his cousin Ciore had unconsciously destroyed the family documents, Bonaccorso had to reconstruct the family history by perusing his grandfather's papers, official documents such as lists of priors, and above all the family's own accounts. For the composition and structure of Bonaccorso's manuscript, see my essay "Per il testo dei ricordi di Bonaccorso Pitti," in *Filologia e critica* X (1985).

Introduction

culture, and was a friend of the famous humanist Coluccio Salutati, whom he supplied with books.

Bonaccorso explicitly stated that he began to write in order to assert the legitimacy — indeed, the right — of his family to participate in running the state, during a period in which the Pitti family's position in the Florentine ruling class was being strongly contested, especially by the Ricasoli family. As Pandimiglio has clearly shown, Bonaccorso's book began "with the intention of being a sort of political manifesto of the Pitti family . . . Apart from specific single scenes, there are two threads that are particularly worthy of note: financial affairs, and especially intra-familiar transactions; and the gradual emergence of Bonaccorso as a point of reference not only for his own family, but for the families of his brothers as well . . ."[38] Thus, a book that was written for political and family reasons, to instruct and admonish the younger members of the clan, "so that you, our children and descendants . . . will take heed of what happens to those who attempt any defense, however reasonable, against someone who is greater and more powerful than they," concludes with an account of the family's reconciliation with the Ricasoli clan. This passionate interest in strengthening one's own clan — also through purchases of property and ecclesiastical benefices — was always present and predominant for Bonaccorso, even during the long years when he was away from Florence, having adventures all over Europe.

Bonaccorso's diary, clearly intended to exalt his own family and to promote its position within the oligarchy of the great Florentine families, goes beyond the canonical lines of this type of literature, at times touching with narrative success on diverse perspectives. Like the composition and structure of the book itself, these episodes revolve around two broad themes that occasionally intersect: the ancient origins and honorable ancestry of the Pitti family and the autobiographical account of Bonaccorso's commercial and political adventures all over Europe, which takes up some sixty pages of the book.

---

38. In "Casa e famiglia: ricordanze fiorentine," *La cultura* (1985).

Introduction

The particular charm of Bonaccorso Pitti's writings can be seen especially in certain lively episodes from his early life; in quality of writing and insight, Pitti is second only to Morelli in these passages, which have a strongly autobiographical nature that is more energetic and enterprising than analytical or meditative.

Bonaccorso's ties with his home in Florence — but not with his family — were somewhat loosened in his early years by the death of his father and by financial difficulties that led the twenty-year-old, "young and inexperienced," to roam the world "and seek my fortune." This decision was contrary to the sedentary, cautious, Florence-centric tendencies of the merchants of that period (as we have seen in the writings of Dati, Niccolini, and Morelli). Added to this spirit of adventure was Bonaccorso's rejection of the populism of the Ciompi and the artisan class; hence he began his wanderings all over Europe.

Bonaccorso is also distinguished from the other diarists by his aristocratic consciousness of his family and of life itself, which made him adverse to a certain mentality and to a certain middle-class narrow-mindedness that predominate in many merchant diaries. He had a strong sense of pride in the Guelf "aristocracy," including the Buondelmonti and Frescobaldi families, which had already risen to the heights of power during the last quarter of the thirteenth century, taking an active role in credit transactions, banking, and the wool trade. Even when he was wheeling and dealing, or gambling, Bonaccorso felt himself to be the rightful heir of his knightly, mysterious ancestor, Bonsignore, who had departed for the Holy Land and disappeared without a trace. Bonaccorso always showed a conservative spirit, disdainful of "new people" and their upheavals against "the good and honor of our State."

Bonaccorso was a genial "merchant of fortune" in the society of the late Middle Ages. He could just as well have been a soldier of fortune, as he could have been a bold knight-errant centuries before. He roamed through the world of European merchants, had encounters with Germans and Frenchmen, with Jews and Levantines, with Genoese and Venetians, cleverly competing with them like a military commander or a knight in a joust. Even his love life had a gallant, chivalrous bent to it — a far cry from the homely middle-class tone of the other merchant writers. He fell in love with a lady named Gemma, a widow; at her command he took off for Rome through the war-torn countryside, as his ancestor had departed for the Holy Land, like a knight taking up a challenge for his lady-love, who in this case mocked him for undertaking such a foolish escapade.

After gambling and losing disastrously, Bonaccorso consoled himself by dancing with a pretty young stranger, who said to him: "Come and dance, Lombard; don't fret over your losses, for God will surely help you."[39] He never felt inferior to the nobles with whom he consorted at the courts of France and Burgundy. After being insulted by the Viscount of Meaux, a relative of the king, Bonaccorso challenged him to a duel, finally obtaining satisfaction from the king himself. Unlike Dati and Morelli, who were cautiously penurious, Bonaccorso loved to wear beautiful clothes, to ride fine horses, to carry splendid weapons, to boast of his wealth and lordly homes, to spend and to lend money generously — all with a late Gothic sensibility and a subtle nostalgia for the gallant days of chivalry.

Although Bonaccorso's behavior did not conform with that of the other *mercatores* of his time, for all its temerity and differentness it was still inspired by the *ragion di mercatura*, which was also, as we have seen, *ragion di famiglia*. The young Bonaccorso realized that because of the precarious situation of his family, which at his father's death had been left without a head, he had to act with extraordinary personal commitment and with new means, as demanded by the new times: the time of a Europe composed of nations, of an Italy torn asunder by hegemonic ambitions, of a capitalistic regime in Florence dominated by a few powerful families. He sensed that he needed to act quickly and unscrupulously, using systematic gambling as well as commerce and trading, and exploiting political power for economic gain. Then, when he had achieved a certain level of credit and financial and social stability,

---

39. "Lombard," i.e., someone from Northern Italy.

he could also invest heavily in real estate and in public funds; he could return to farming and manufacturing, in which his father had made considerable sums, and could become part of the new oligarchic system in Florence by holding public office.

After sixteen years away from Florence, Bonaccorso returned with a wife and children in 1396 to settle down in his native city and become a fixture in the ruling class. Finally, after the republic was restored in 1382, there was again a ruling class in Florence, now made up of upper middle-class merchants and friends and colleagues of the Pitti family.[40] Between 1395 and 1396, the political group led by Maso degli Albizzi (one of whose nieces was Bonaccorso's wife) gained more and more power in the Florentine state, effecting a foreign policy favorable to France, where Bonaccorso could be very useful on account of his many connections.

But whether he was rambling around Europe or rooted in his native Florence, Bonaccorso's fundamental commitment was to his business and to his family. "A daring gambler" is how an anonymous diarist described him in 1386, at the time when Bonaccorso was already carrying out an important early commission in the Piazza della Signoria.[41] But as a gambler, Bonaccorso was never dangerous or maniacal, casual or frivolous. He was a systematic, technical gambler, professional and organized. Here, too, he was a "merchant" — a sort of precursor of the entrepreneurs of today's gambling casinos. For Bonaccorso, gambling was a commercial enterprise, like lending or exchanging money, in which one had to win through skill and caution, without complaining when one lost because one deserved to lose.

Gambling was clearly Bonaccorso's ruling passion from the time of his first big European *quête* in Slavonia and Hungary in 1379. These are perhaps his most lively, animated pages, dominated by the reckless, exuberant character of Bonaccorso the protagonist — reminiscent of Cellini, it has been said. Against the

---

40. After the aristocracy and the Guelfs overthrew the government of the Ciompi, the Florentine republic was restored.

41. Alessandro Gherardi, ed. *Diario d'anonimo fiorentino dall'anno 1358 al 1389* (Florence, 1876), p. 466.

Introduction

squallid, ruthless backdrop of speculators and moneylenders reminiscent of Boccaccio's Ser Ciappelletto, we see Bonaccorso and his Florentine friends amid exotic sights and sounds, constantly gambling on the market and on life itself.

For Bonaccorso Pitti, gambling gradually became not only a source of fresh money for investments and business deals, from saffron to horses to wool to wine and foodstuffs, from precious metals and fabrics to jewels and even loans and usury; it also became a way to make connections — on an increasingly high social level — especially with the courts of Charles VI of France and Louis II of Anjou. Bonaccorso played the role of the organizer of gambling sessions in various princely settings. After 1396, having acted as the agent for several other big gambling entrepreneurs, and taking some big risks, Bonaccorso refused to become directly entangled in such matters except on the very highest level and in truly exceptional cases involving princes and other royals who could be of advantage in his strategy of public relations in favor of himself and the Florentine state. This was the new road down which Bonaccorso had started in order to move the art of being a merchant toward new successes in the new Italian and European situation.

What had been negative behavior for Paolo da Certaldo and for Boccaccio at the beginning of the fourteenth century — that is, gambling and consorting with the great for one's own personal gain — was now chosen by Bonaccorso within the context of the new socio-political reality as the best way to establish himself quickly and solidly; Morelli was still against this. Along with money from gambling, Bonaccorso also received gifts and prebends from popes and cardinals, kings and princes, often for political motives or as compensation for services rendered (middleman, informer, lobbyist for the interests of Florence at the papal court, etc.). Money also flowed in as a result of special privileges that more or less gave him a monopoly on certain things. Another way up the ladder to the Florentine oligarchy was through diplomatic activity; and this political advancement was now necessary

---

42. The Medici were allies of the Pitti family.

Introduction

for acquiring financial power in Florence, as Lorenzo de' Medici would realize years later.[42]

Gambling, being in favor with the great and powerful, diplomatic missions and government appointments all required an exquisitely personal touch, an eminently individual activity — or rather, activism. Acting on behalf of one's family or of one's company (be it in banking, trading, or production) would be inappropriate, perhaps even counterproductive and certainly unnecessary in the context of this new political and economic strategy for gaining power.

Bonaccorso's activities, indeed his entire life and hence his writings, which mirror his life, cannot help being of a highly personal nature: they were all focused on and emanated from his strong personality; hence his writing has an obsessively ecocentric quality. Bonaccorso's "I" dominates uncontested, from the insistent, sonorous formula "I, Bonaccorso" which, placed at the usual pious, canonical invocation, begins both parts of his memoirs and punctuates the crucial moments of the narration. And that "I" is also present in the structure and language of his work, which are admittedly very mercantile in character, but with a persistent new egotistical slant. The powerful, implacable presence of Bonaccorso's own personality, his arrogant will to lord it over everyone and everything, his constant perception of himself as the architect of his own success (to the point of ostentatious boasting) were certainly the strongest and most efficacious stimuli for him as a writer. They have even led some critics to see in Bonaccorso's autobiographical writings a foreshadowing of the heroic self-projection of Benvenuto Cellini a century and a half later.

In Buda as in Paris, in Avignon as in London, in Costanza as in Rotterdam, what Bonaccorso saw amid the crowds of people (at least when he was narrating the story) was principally himself, or whatever interested him directly. He focused on the "frightening, cruel" sight (akin to Manzoni's depiction of the plague in Milan) of a mother and her three sons burned alive in a house to which soldiers set fire in the Hundred Years' War, in order to emphasize his own presence and his own sufferings and the risks he ran during the invasion of Picardy in 1383. He recalled even his first important public office (as a member of the Eight on Security) in passing, as a pretext for pointing out his own courage when the Public Palace was struck by lightning and he was injured.[43] He wrote enthusiastically only about himself and what directly concerned him, although he generally wrote about historical events with a degree of precision, as Léon Mirot and Gene Brucker have shown. The only times he erred in making historical or political assessments were precisely on account of the distorting effect of his own interests and personal reactions.

In every place and every circumstance, Bonaccorso lived and acted, as Bec has observed, not to *see*, but to *do* — to do things himself and to write about himself and what interested him above all as a *mercator*, to add to his wealth. The whole series of wanderings and extraordinary adventures that Bonaccorso had in the most diverse countries of Europe, alongside powerful figures (emperors and kings, princes and dukes, popes and cardinals, soldiers of fortune and government ministers) over a long span of years concludes with his return to Florence, seen in a totally financial light: "I found that I had 10,000 gold francs worth of wool, as well as a house and chattels and horses and equipment, not counting about five thousand francs in cash."

For a writer with such an egocentric perspective, it is natural that the most lively, expressive moments should be self-portraits or self-descriptions in the course of the most varied adventures and circumstances, always resolutely in action, always realistically energetic. At times Bonaccorso depicts himself quite boastfully; other times his tone is disenchanted and even self-ironic. The two perspectives alternate quite effectively.

Bonaccorso was a hero who, when he wrote about himself, not only wanted to always be the center of attention, but also to be indefatigably in action, provoking actions and reactions, bringing things rapidly to a conclusion. Proud of his ability to move swiftly — and therefore profitably — throughout Europe, Bonaccorso saw swiftness of decision and of action as a *sine qua*

---

43. The *Otto di Guardia* was the Florentine commission for state security.

non of success. "Long before Machiavelli," notes Bec, "Bonaccorso was reproaching his fellow Florentines, as well as the French, for their procrastinations. A man totally bent on action, Bonaccorso used gestures rather than words." Like Machiavelli, Bonaccorso wrote in short, incisive sentences, with no paraphrases or discursive flourishes, going straight to the facts, indeed often cutting explanations short with brief or allusive sayings, or even with inelegant but expeditious expressions like *etc., etc.,* or by referring to preceding words or actions.

This is how Bonaccorso lived his life: with no pauses for reflection or doubts or debate. The time of his narration is the time of the action, an action that always takes place with strict, inexorable logic. Without action, the account itself becomes feeble and vague.

Even in the work of a writer as exhibitionistic as Bonaccorso, autobiography was still a more or less important element — albeit the most lively and efficacious from an expressive point of view — of the *ragion di mercatura* and *ragion di famiglia*. For Bonaccorso, in spite of his egocentricity and his cosmopolitanism, the family and the patrimony — and the city of Florence, as the family of families — remained the overarching, constantly recurring points of reference in the midst of all his personal escapades and all the complex situations of the Europe of his day. If at the beginning of Bonaccorso's diary, in the usual invocation to God for the prosperity of the family, the "I" is missing, it returns unremittingly throughout the rest of the work, even in the most traditional interweaving of God and gain (e.g., "as you can see, more through good fortune or by the grace of God, than through talent or intelligence"; or "be comforted in the hope of God and in useful actions"). Not by chance, Bonaccorso's diary, like his last will and testament, concludes with an act of confidence and piety toward the Virgin Mary.

Several diaries from the fifteenth and early sixteenth centuries were also written with the traditional approach, in which the

Introduction

vocation of the merchant and his devotion to his family were pursued under the protection of divine providence. The families in these cases are exemplary: the Palmieri, Rucellai, Landucci, Masi, Corsini, Capponi, Machiavelli, Medici, Guicciardini.

Thanks to their activities as merchants and their land holdings in the Val di Pesa, the Machiavelli also participated in the regime of the moneyed middle class. Although he had studied law and participated in public office, Bernardo di Niccolò spent most of his energies as a good, parsimonious steward of his own not extensive property, attempting not only to buy and sell products of the land and fabrics but also to profit from the very newest objects of commerce, books.[45] Bernardo had the tightfisted, hairsplitting nature of the second generation of Florentine merchants, who were more deeply rooted in their native city than the first; but he was open to the new art of printing, in which he also participated professionally, compiling indices. Bernardo's wholly Florentine spirit, which took pleasure in local gossip and scandals — like Sacchetti, Velluti, and later Poliziano in the *Detti* — is expressed in the novellistic slant of his story of the affair of the servant girl. In the end, Bernardo's story of his relative's affair with the maidservant takes on a financial dimension when he describes the indemnifications and investments in the Dowry Fund made on behalf of the pregnant girl. For Bernardo, the traditional attention to his children's education as a guarantee of the family's continued prosperity focused on the selection of good teachers and good texts; but he was also careful to note them in his ledger of expenditures. It is particularly interesting to observe how closely Bernardo followed his son Niccolò not only in his studies, but also in his first small commercial assignments. Like one of the gaily garbed, courtly young boys who make their appearance in

---

45. Bernardo di Niccolò di Buoninsegna Machiavelli (1428–1500), a doctor of jurisprudence, treasurer and jurisconsult. In 1458 he married Bartolomea Nelli, the widow of Niccolò Benizzi, and had two daughters with her, Primavera and Margherita, and two sons, Niccolò (born May 3, 1469) and Totto. He occupied himself chiefly with managing the estate he had inherited from his uncle Totto, operating as an agrarian merchant.

Introduction

the frescoes of Ghirlandaio and Benozzo Gozzoli, the seven-year-old Niccolò appears for the first time in his father's diary in an elegant little tunic and cloak. We see Niccolò again at the age of 17 or 18, in "long, dark purplish-blue hose," helping his father in small transactions. Bernardo paid for the binding of Livy's *Decades* with three flasks of red wine and a flask of vinegar; his punctilious notes seem to envelop — indeed, to predestine — Niccolò amid agrarian and commercial dealings: lambs and cheeses, asses and oxen, piglets and capons, grains and wine, olive oil and vinegar, textile manufacturing on a modest scale. His was a world of small-scale financial investments — in public funds and private loans, and purchases of legal, historical, and literary texts (he bought all of Livy, in fact), which he completed with indices, had bound, and then re-sold. Ancient and modern books (including Biondo Flavio[46]) are mentioned in the same breath with red wine, cheeses, and fabrics to be woven or cut and sewn into various articles of clothing. Bernardo's considerations and reflections on the great classical texts and historical events or the vicissitudes of the Florentine state are interspersed with observations on the humble, realistic necessities and experiences of everyday life — eating and drinking, growing crops and caring for livestock, trying to avoid taxes and forced loans, keeping precise records of debits and credits.

Earlier in the century, Giovanni di Pagolo Morelli had admonished his son to "study Virgil, Boethius, Seneca or other authors for at least an hour every day;" and he quoted from the scriptures, Dante, and even Boccaccio. Study and meditation were not merely a source of consolation and spiritual comfort for the Florentine merchants; they were also a guide for living, a source of action beyond the Ciceronian *topos* of man's "relationship" with books. Niccolò Machiavelli wrote about "that food which is mine alone" (i.e., the classics of ancient literature) at the time he was writing *The Prince*, while also mentioning his humble occupations in the

---

46. Also known as Flavius Blondus (Forlì 1392–Rome 1463), a humanist and historian who is credited with inventing the notion of the "Middle Ages." Niccolò Machiavelli consulted Flavio Biondo for his analysis of the disunity of Italy.

Introduction

country, and the hours he spent at the local tavern. But, as already noted, for a solid merchant like Morelli, what realistically mattered more than "the ancient courts of men of old" was above all the direct experience of "the most material things" — that is, "long experience of modern affairs." More than eighty years later, this is what Niccolò Machiavelli explicitly echoed in his introduction to *The Prince*.

In spite of the different commercial and banking situations more than half a century after Bernardo's time, and in spite of the fact that Niccolò Machiavelli boasted that he knew nothing about financial matters, the author of *The Prince* was always aware of the practical domestic and commercial issues that had accompanied the political and economic tumult in Florence since the mid-fourteenth century. Those tumultuous events were recounted not only by the historians who came after Villani,[47] but also in the homely diaries of the Florentine middle class of the fourteenth and fifteenth centuries, as they did in Bernardo's. As Morelli eloquently reveals, they were inspired above all by the most ordinary, everyday political, economic, and social experiences rather than by intellectual or abstract reflections.

In the Florentine diaries of the early Medici period, divine providence and its minister, Fortune, still predominated over "virtue"— in an anti-Machiavellian way. "By the fortune and grace of God," was an insistent formula in Bonaccorso Pitti and the diarists who came after him. (In his *Canzone morale* Bonaccorso wrote that "With the free will granted by God, man can take the good path . . . fortune is good or bad, depending upon what Providence does. . . .") Bec rightly points out that even Pitti's activism was regulated by the rule of never tempting fate or acting against divine providence.

In the diaries of the Florentine High Renaissance, even in the

---

47. The post-Villani historians have recently been studied by Matucci in relation to Machiavelli.

ones written by the strongest personalities up to and including Guicciardini, annotations and narrations usually had as their point of departure domestic and professional records rooted in practical everyday realities. Like the diaries of the two preceding centuries, they were inspired by the most ordinary experiences.

It was precisely on account of this immediate realism that the *ragion di Stato* theorized by Giovanni Botero[48] began to make inroads on the *ragion di mercatura* and *ragion di famiglia* that had dominated Florentine diaries until the early fifteenth century. But it had already clearly manifested itself in the writings of Bonaccorso Pitti and Giovanni Rucellai. As we have seen, merchants were becoming increasingly involved in politics; economic power and political power were becoming intertwined. "The State was governed more from behind the merchants' counters than from the Public Palace," observed Giovanni Cavalcanti at mid-century.[49] The Florentine state had been put into a situation of crisis by the powerful families and their princes — including Lorenzo de' Medici, who began his own diary with considerations of a wholly politico-economic nature. By this time, the state had taken the place of the large family of families from the politically engaged middle class that had run Florence in former times. This new driving force — the State — converging with the impulse to make money, would soon spring into the foreground and impose itself in a more absolute way, like a true Machiavellian prince. And the figure of the prince became increasingly dominant as an example — not in an abstract or heroic way, but based on a direct experience of civic life, notwithstanding the obligatory references to classical antiquity: "if you should reach the highest level [of the State], then I would advise you to strive to resemble our Roman forefathers, for as we are descended from them in essence, we should show this in virtue and substance as well," Morelli had admonished his son a century earlier.

---

48. Giovanni Botero (1549–1617), the Piedmontese thinker who enunciated the law of increase of population later known as Malthus' Law. Botero's *Della ragione di Stato* was published for the first time in Venice in 1589.

49. *Istorie fiorentine* II, 1.

Introduction

Lorenzo de' Medici wrote his *ricordi* for his sons, of course, but in their role of those who would inherit his political power ("for the enlightenment and information of those who shall come after").[50] The writer-prince Lorenzo remembered his forefathers, but focused most of all on his grandfather Cosimo as a model of the family-state concept. More than the account of a family, Lorenzo's is the story of a dynasty, both ascending and descending. From the very beginning, his diary, rather like Bonaccorso Pitti's, is dominated by the egotism of the narrating "I" who relegates the family genealogy to later pages: "I find in our father Piero's writings that I was born on the first of January 1448 . . ."

Even Lorenzo's attention to the economic status of the Medici dynasty was inspired by the *ragion di Stato* more than the *ragion di mercatura* or *ragion di famiglia* — a State that represented first and foremost wealth and economic power. "I accepted unwillingly the reins of the city and the State, as my grandfather and father had done, but only to safeguard our friends and our wealth, because it is difficult to live as a rich man in Florence without the support of the State." Lorenzo, who identified with the State, did not truly have day-to-day experience as a merchant, and had never worked behind a counter; his was a world of government and culture, absolutely dominated by the *ragion di Stato*. Rather like the other great statesman — Niccolò Machiavelli — Lorenzo was cut off from the everyday work of the *mercatores* (although he had some merchants in his family), detached from the cult of family and city, dazzled by the new reality of the State ("Since I cannot speak about silk or wool, nor about gains and losses, I must either vow to keep quiet or speak about the State," wrote Machiavelli to Francesco Vettori on April 9, 1913). But Machiavelli's paradigmatic prince, Cesare Borgia, still bears some resemblance to the Gian Galeazzo Visconti depicted by Morelli, Dati, and Pitti.

---

50. They seem to be the continuation of an uninterrupted series of family diaries begun in 1360 by Foligno di Conte de' Medici. Of course given the particular situation of "The Magnificent" Lorenzo de' Medici, his section represents a unique case.

Introduction

In his *Memorie di famiglia* and *Ricordanze*[51] Giovanni Guicciardini seemed to be inspired by a more traditionally "mercantile" vision, along the lines of Velluti's and Morelli's family/moral/social diaries. Guicciardini seems to recall these earlier diarists even in his initial pious invocation and in his punctilious recountings of oral histories, in his admonishments to secrecy, in his lists of purchases and of debtors and creditors, in his complacent recording of his own *cursus honorum* and that of his family. Guicciardini begins his family history like this:

> I have written this family history with great toil and diligence, not so much from the things I have heard as from my own memory, and much more from letters . . . And because I shall be totally truthful here, I beg our descendants, to whom this history will be handed down, not to show it to anyone outside of the family, but to keep it for their own use, for I have written it solely for that reason . . .

He adds, sonorously:

> . . . I desire two things above everything else in the world: one is the perpetual exhaltation of this city and its liberty, and the other is the glory of our family, not only during my lifetime, but in perpetuity. May it please God to preserve and enrich both.[52]

The conception of the family as the nucleus of the city and the State, as the family of families, and the presentation of one's forefathers in function of their participation in public life were both the main idea and the narrative method that dominated and characterized the most important diaries of the Florentine merchants of the fourteenth and fifteenth centuries. Guicciardini clearly took up that idea and that method. He spoke about his native Florence with an almost mystical, providential devotion, as a temple of justice and liberty worthy of a final invocation to God, as Morelli had already done.

The literary tradition which, from the chronicles and ethic-civic

---

51. Published in volume IX of *Opere inedite*, edited by G. Canestrini (Florence, 1857), and in *Scritti autobiografici e rari di Francesco Guicciardini*, edited by R. Palmarocchi (Bari, 1936).
52. *Scritti autobiografici e rari di Francesco Guicciardini*, p. 3.

treatises of the time of Dante had blossomed into the complex, lively autobiographical genre of Lorenzo de' Medici, Machiavelli, and Cellini and thence to the great historiograhic and political works of sixteenth-century Florence — from Giannotti to Guicciardini — remains far from the proposals of abstract perfection, ideal models, and masterpieces advanced and longed for by the most famous of the Renaissance writers of precepts, from Bembo to Castiglione to Della Casa. Rather, these are diaries filtered day by day through a deeply felt moral reflection, keen and indefatigable in Morelli and unparalleled in any of his contemporaries, except perhaps by Neri di Gino Capponi on the political level.[53]

It is true that the middle-class Florentine merchants of the fourteenth and fifteenth centuries no longer had the open, adventurous spirit of their forefathers. But they were nourished by a spiritual and cultural experience, by a pondered human knowledge which, if it did not permit them to act with the temerity of their fathers, did make them aware of the values of history and the constant misery of man. If the aggressive merchant paladins had been the protagonists of the young, audacious civilization of Dante and Boccaccio, Arnolfo di Cambio and Giotto, then the merchants of the following age with their books of thoughtful moral and civic *ricordi* were the exemplars of the more reflective, mature civilization of the Florentine Quattrocento. They were the forerunners of the taste for the concrete, the discriminating, the overarching cautiousness, the melancholy, deeply human moral discourse of Francesco Guicciardini.

---

53. Neri di Gino Capponi (1388–1457), a prominent Florentine statesman who wrote *Commentari dell'acquisto di Pisa*; see *Cronichette antiche di vari scrittori del buon secolo della lingua toscana*, Domenico Maria Manni, ed. (Milan, 1844).

Bibliographic Note

The foregoing introduction, as well as the selection of texts and the compilation of the footnotes, are the result of my studies of the "merchant writers" over a period of almost fifty years, beginning with those that first sparked my interest in this genre: "Per il testo del *Decameron*," in *Studi di filologia italiana* VIII (1950); my edition of Giovanni Morelli's *Ricordi* (Florence, 1956); "L'epopea dei mercanti," in *Lettere italiane* VIII, 1956. I was stimulated above all by the pioneering studies of Christian Bec suggested by Fernand Braudel (*Les marchands écrivains*, Paris, 1967, and *Les livres des florentins*, Florence, 1984), as well as several other contributions; Gene Brucker's *Florentine Politics and Society* (Princeton, 1962), and *The Diaries of Bonaccorso Pitti and Gregorio Dati*, (New York, 1967; translation by Julia Martines); Leonida Pandimiglio's study suggested by Arsenio Frugoni, "Casa e famiglia: ricordanze fiorentine," in *La cultura* (1985) and various studies on Morelli in *Studi sul Medioevo cristiano* (Rome, 1974) and *Studi medievali* series 3, vol. xxii (1981), and many other fundamental writings.

These pages also derive from my more recent, systematic works: *Mercanti Scrittori* (Milan, 1986-87) and *Con amore volere: narrar di mercatanti fra Boccaccio e Machiavelli* (Venice, 1996). These

Bibliographic Note

two volumes contain extensive, specific references and bibliographic citations that I will not repeat here (at times I refer to them simply by the author's name).

Nevertheless, I will indicate several works that provide a general framework (especially ones written in or translated into English): Amintore Fanfani, *Le origini dello spirito capitalistico in Italia* (Milan, 1933); Max Weber, *The Protestant Ethic and the Spirit of Capitalism* (New York, 1976; translated from the German by Talcott Parsons); Yves Renouard, *Les hommes d'affaires italiens du Moyen Age* (Paris, 1949); Michael M. Postan and Edwin E. Rich, eds., *Trade and Industry in the Middle Ages* (Cambridge, 1952; second edition, 1987); Lauro Martines, *The Social World of the Florentine Humanists* (Princeton, 1963) and *Power and Imagination: City-States in Renaissance Italy* (New York, 1979); Armando Sapori, *Studi di storia economica* (Florence, 1995; 3 vols.), *La mercatura medievale* (Florence, 1972), and *The Italian Merchant in the Middle Ages* (New York, 1970; translated from the Italian by Patricia Ann Kennen); Robert Sabatino Lopez, *The Birth of Europe* (New York, 1967); Vittore Branca, "The Mercantile Epic," in *Boccaccio : The Man and His Works* (New York, 1976; translated by Richard Monges); Alberto Tenenti, "Les marchands et la culture," in *Annales ESC* XXIII (1968); Georges Duby and Jacques Le Goff, eds., *Famille et parenté dans l'Occident* (Paris, 1977); David Herlihy and Christiane Klapisch-Zuber, *Tuscans And Their Families: a Study of the Florentine Catasto of 1427* (New Haven, 1985); Carlo M. Cipolla, *Il fiorino e il quattrino: la politica monetaria a Firenze nel Trecento* (Bologna, 1982); Angelo Cicchetti and Raul Mordenti, *I libri di famiglia in Italia* (Rome, 1985); Anthony Molho, *Marriage Alliance in Late Medieval Florence* (Cambridge, MA, 1994).

The texts for the translations that appear on the following pages were taken from the following editions:

Giovanni Boccaccio, *Decameron*, Vittore Branca, editor (Turin: Einaudi, 12th edition, 1997).

Bibliographic Note

Giovanni Boccaccio, *Epistole*, G. Auzzas, editor, vol. I of *Tutte le opere di Giovanni Boccaccio*, Vittore Branca, general editor (Milan: Mondadori, 1992).

Domenico Lenzi, *Specchio umano*, in G. Pinto, *Il libro del Biadaiolo* (Florence: Olschki, 1978).

Paolo da Certaldo, *Libro di buoni costumi*, S. Morpurgo, editor (Florence: Le Monnier, 1921; reproduced in the 1945 edition by Alfredo Schiaffini).

Giovanni di Pagolo Morelli, *Ricordi*, Vittore Branca, editor (Florence: Le Monnier, 1956; 1969^2).

Bonaccorso Pitti, *Ricordi*, in *Mercanti scrittori*, Vittore Branca, editor (Milan: Rusconi, 1986, 1987^3).

Donato Velluti, *Ricordi*, in *Mercanti scrittori*.

Goro Dati, *Il libro segreto*, in *Mercanti scrittori*.

Francesco Datini, *Testamento*, in *Lettere di un notaro a un mercante del secolo XIV*, Cesare Guasti, editor, and in *Mercanti scrittori*.

Lapo Niccolini de' Sirigatti, *Libro degli affari propri*, Christian Bec, editor (Paris: S.E.V.P.E.N., 1969).

Bernardo Machiavelli, *Libro di ricordi*, Cesare Olschki, editor (Florence: Le Monnier, 1954).

Niccolò Machiavelli, *Lettera al Vettori* in *Tutte le opere*, Mario Martelli, editor (Florence: Sansoni, 1971).

Lorenzo de' Medici, *Opere*, Tiziano Zanato, editor (Turin: Einaudi, 1992).

Merchant Writers

Giovanni Boccaccio

Decameron DAY II, TALE 5

Andreuccio of Perugia, having come to Naples to buy horses, has three grave misadventures in one night, escapes from all of them, and returns home with a ruby.

'Landolfo's stones' — began Fiammetta, whose turn it was to tell a tale — 'have reminded me of a story no less full of perils than the one told by Lauretta, yet different from hers, in which the misadventures took place over several years, while in mine they occurred in a single night, as you shall hear.

According to what I once heard, there was in Perugia a young man whose name was Andreuccio di Pietro, a horse trader. Having heard that there was a good market for horses in Naples, he put five hundred gold florins in a purse and, never having been away from home, departed for Naples with some other traders. He arrived on a Sunday evening around the hour of vespers and having been informed by his landlord where the market square was, he went there the next morning. Andreuccio saw many horses he liked, and haggled a good deal, but couldn't strike a bargain. And to show that he had truly come to buy, he took out the purse full of florins several times in front of the people who were coming and going, for he was inexperienced and incautious.

As he was thus bargaining, and having shown his purse, it happened that a young Sicilian woman, very beautiful but willing to satisfy any man for a small price, passed near Andreuccio, without his noticing her. She saw his purse and immediately said to herself: "Who would be better off than I, if that money were mine?" and walked on. There was with this girl an old woman, also Sicilian, who after seeing Andreuccio and letting the young woman walk on, rushed up to embrace him affectionately. Seeing this, the young woman went off to one side to observe her, without saying a thing. Turning to the old woman and recognizing her, Andreuccio greeted her joyously. Promising to come to him where he was staying, the old woman left without holding too much discourse with him there. Andreuccio went back to bargaining, but bought nothing that morning. The young woman, who had first seen Andreuccio's purse and his acquaintance with the old woman, discreetly began to ask who he was and where he was from, and how the old woman knew him, to see if there were any way she could get all or part of his money. The old woman told her in detail about Andreuccio, almost as he himself would have done; for she had dwelt a long time in his father's household in Sicily and later in Perugia. She also recounted where he was from and why he had come.

Now fully informed about Andreuccio's family and their names, the young woman made a plan to satisfy her greed with a cunning trick. Returning home, she gave the old woman so much to do that day that she could not go to see Andreuccio. And toward evening she sent a servant girl of hers, whom she had trained well in such services, to the place where Andreuccio was staying.

When the servant girl arrived at the inn, she happened to find Andreuccio himself standing in the doorway alone, and asked him where she might find Andreuccio of Perugia. When he said that he was Andreuccio, she took him aside and said: "Sir, if you please, a gentle lady of this place would fain speak with you." Andreuccio, who considered himself a handsome young man, decided that the lady must be in love with him — as if she could find no other comely young men in Naples save himself — and promptly replied that he was ready to wait upon her, and asked where and when this lady wished to speak to him, to which the girl replied: "Sir, whenever you may be pleased to come, she awaits you in her house."

Without saying a word to anyone at the inn, Andreuccio replied: "Go on ahead, I shall come after you." So the girl led him to the house of the young woman, who lived in a quarter called the Malpertugio, which is as respectable a place as its name indicates.[1] But Andreuccio, who neither knew nor suspected any of this, thinking he was going to a reputable place to see an amiable lady, followed the girl into the house. The girl had already called to her mistress and said, "Andreuccio is here," as they were going up the stairs, and he saw her appear at the top of the stairs to receive him.

She was still a very young woman, tall, with a beautiful face, dressed and bedecked very respectably. As soon as Andreuccio approached her, she took three steps down toward him with her arms open wide; then throwing her arms around his neck she said nothing for a while, as if she were overcome by emotion; then, weeping, she kissed his forehead and said in a broken voice: "O my Andreuccio, you are welcome!" Andreuccio, wondering at such a tender reception, answered, all in amazement: "My lady, you are well met!"

She took him by the hand and led him up to her drawing room and then, without saying another thing, she entered with him into her bedchamber, which smelled of roses, orange blossoms, and other fragrances. There was a beautiful curtained bed there, and many garments hanging on rods, as is the custom in Naples; and he saw many other beautiful, rich furnishings. On account of these things, since he was a stranger, he firmly believed that she was nothing less than a great lady.

They sat down upon a chest at the foot of her bed, and she began to speak to him thus: "Andreuccio, I am quite sure that

---

1. *Malpertugio*, meaning "the evil hole," was an ill-famed neighborhood near the port of Naples.

you wonder at my affectionate greeting, and at my tears, since you don't know me and have never chanced to hear of me. But presently you shall hear something that will make you wonder even more: I am your sister. And I tell you that, since God has granted that before I die I have seen one of my brothers — as I wish I could see you all — I shall not die unconsoled. And if you perhaps never heard this, I want to tell it you. As I believe you know, Pietro, my father and yours, dwelt a long time in Palermo; and on account of his goodness and comely looks, there were and still are those who knew him to be very well loved. But of all those who loved him, my mother — a gentlewoman, at that time a widow — loved him best; so much so that, putting aside her fear of her father and brothers, and even her pride, she became so intimate with him that I was born of it, and am as you see me now. Then when Pietro had to leave Palermo and return to Perugia, he left me, a little girl, with my mother, nor did he ever remember me or her, that I heard of. If he hadn't been my father, I would strongly reproach him for his ingratitude toward my mother, who put all she had, and likewise herself, into his hands, without even knowing who he was, moved by the most faithful love (not to mention the love he should have shown me, a daughter born not of a maidservant nor of a woman of low degree). But what of it? Evil deeds of long ago are far easier to reproach than to remedy; that's how the story went. He left me, a little girl, in Palermo, where when I had grown up almost as you see me now, my mother, who was a rich woman, gave me in marriage to a man from Agrigento — a gentle, upstanding man, who out of love for my mother and me came to live in Palermo. And there, since he is a staunch Guelph,[2] he began to have some dealings with our own King Carlo.[3] But King Federico came to hear of their plans before they could be put into effect; so we had to flee Sicily just when I was expecting to become the greatest lady that had ever been on that island. We took the few things we were able to take with us (few, I say, compared to the many we had), left our

---

2. See note 8 to Giovanni di Pagolo Morelli, p. 57.
3. King Carlo is Charles II (ca. 1254–1309) of Naples; King Federico is Frederick III, King of Sicily from 1296 until his death in 1337.

lands and palaces, and took refuge here in Naples, where we found King Carlo to be so grateful to us that he compensated us for some of the losses we had suffered on his account. He has given us land and houses, and continues to give a good stipend to my husband, who is your brother-in-law, as you shall have occasion to see. And that is how, sweet my brother, I came to be here, where thanks to God's mercy and not your own, I see you." And thus saying, she embraced him again, and again weeping kissed him tenderly on the forehead.

Hearing her tell this story in such a precise way, with such composure (for she never hesitated or stumbled over her words), and remembering that it was true that his father had been in Palermo, and knowing, as a young man himself, how young men are (for when they are young, they love easily), and seeing her tender tears, embraces, and chaste kisses, Andreuccio took what she said as more than true. When she had finished her story, he answered her: "My lady, you must not think it strange that I am amazed. For truly, for whatever reason, my father never spoke of your mother or you; or if he did, it never came to my notice. I had no knowledge of you, as if you did not exist. And it is so much dearer to me to have found you here, my sister, in that I am all alone and I least expected it. And verily I know no man so highly placed that you should not be dear to him, much less to myself, who am a simple horse trader. But I pray you to make one thing clear to me: How did you know I was here?" To which she replied: "I was told this morning by a poor woman who is a retainer of mine; for she tells me that she was long with our father in Palermo and Perugia. And if it weren't that I thought it more seemly for you to come to me here in your own home than that I should go to you in someone else's, I would have come to you straight away."

Then she began to ask him in detail about all of his relatives by name, and Andreuccio answered all her questions. This made him believe even more what he should have believed least.

The talk had been long, and the heat was great; and she called for Greco[4] and sweetmeats and bid Andreuccio drink. After this,

---

4. Common white wine.

he wished to leave, for it was time for supper. She would not hear of this, and, pretending to be greatly upset, embraced him and said: "Woe is me, for I know how little you love me! To think that you are with your sister, whom you have never seen before, and in her home, where you should have laid your bags, and you want to leave to have supper at an inn? Forsooth, you shall dine with me; and because my husband is not here, which grieves me deeply, I shall do my best as a lady to honor you." Andreuccio, not knowing what else to answer, said: "I love you as well as any sister should be loved, but if I don't go, they'll wait supper for me all evening, which would be very discourteous of me." Then she said: "God be praised, if I don't have anyone in the house to send to say that they shouldn't wait for you! Though you would be much more courteous, and would be doing your duty, if you sent to say to your companions that they should come here to dine. Then, should you still want to go away, the whole company of you can leave together."

Andreuccio replied that he didn't want to be with his companions that evening, but that if it would please her, she should do with him as she wished. She then pretended to send to the inn to say that they shouldn't wait for him for supper; then, after much more talk, they sat down to dine and were served splendidly with various dishes. And she slyly drew things out until it was pitch dark. When they got up from the table and Andreuccio made as if to leave, she said that in no wise would she suffer this, since Naples was no place to be going about at night, especially for a stranger; and that just as she had sent to say that they shouldn't wait for him for supper, she had also said that they shouldn't expect him back at the inn to sleep that night. Andreuccio was taken in by this and believed and was pleased by it; so he agreed to stay. Therefore, after supper, they spoke at length on many subjects; and since part of the night had passed, she left Andreuccio to sleep in her bedchamber with a little boy to assist him should he want anything, and went off with her maidservants to another chamber.

The heat was very great; so once he was alone, Andreuccio removed his doublet and hose and hung them over the head of the bed. And feeling the natural urge to void the excess weight from his belly, he asked the boy where that was done. The boy showed him a door in a corner of the room and said, "Go in there." The gullible Andreuccio went in, and happening to put his foot down on a board that lay crosswise over a beam, the board tipped over, taking him down with it. God loved him so well that in spite of how far he had fallen he wasn't injured at all, but he was totally covered with the filth with which the place was full. I want to describe this place to you so that you can better understand what I've said as well as what is to come. It was in a narrow space, as we often see between two houses. The place to sit down upon was on two boards placed between the two houses with boards set across them; it was one of these boards that had fallen, taking Andreuccio with it.

Finding himself down in the pit, poor Andreuccio began to call for the boy. But as soon as he had heard him fall, the boy had run to tell the lady. She, running to her bedchamber, immediately looked to see if any of Andreuccio's clothes were there. She found the clothes and with them the money, which out of distrust Andreuccio foolishly always carried with him. Now that she had the thing on which she, a woman from Palermo pretending to be the sister of a man from Perugia, had set her sights, she thought no more of him, but closed the door through which he had passed before he fell.

When the boy didn't answer him, Andreuccio began to call out more loudly, but to no avail. Now suspecting — too late — that he had been duped, he climbed over the low wall that enclosed the pit, and went down into the street. He went to the door of the house, which he well recognized, and for a long time he called and shook the door and pounded on it. Now clearly seeing his misfortune, he wept, saying: "Woe is me, in what a short time have I lost five hundred florins and a sister!"

After many more words, he started all over again to pound on the door and to shout, to such a degree that many of the neighbors awoke, unable to tolerate the disturbance, and got out of bed. And one of the lady's maidservants, looking very sleepy, came to the window and said in a scolding voice: "Who is knocking down there?"

"Oh!" said Andreuccio, "Don't you know me? I am Andreuccio, the brother of Madonna Fiordaliso." To which she replied: "Good man, if you've had too much to drink, get you to bed and come back tomorrow morning; I know no Andreuccio nor what tales these are you tell. Go now, and let us sleep, if you please."

"What?" said Andreuccio, "Don't you understand what I'm saying? Of course you do; but if this is how families treat each other in Sicily, forgetting their relationships in such a short time, at least give me back my clothes, which I left there, and I will willingly go with God."

To which she laughingly replied: "Good man, I think you must be dreaming." Saying this, going back inside, and closing the window were all one. Now certain of his misfortune, Andreuccio was becoming more angry than worried, and almost determined to take back by force what he had been unable to obtain by words. So, picking up a large stone, he began to pound on the door with far stronger blows than before. Many of the neighbors who had awoken and got up before, believing him to be some scoundrel who was feigning in order to annoy that good woman, exasperated by his pounding, came to their windows. And just as all the dogs of a neighborhood will bark at a strange dog, they began to say: "This is a great villainy, to come at this hour to the home of fine ladies and spout such nonsense. Go to! Go with God, good man; let us sleep, if you please. And if you have something to say to her, come back tomorrow. Don't plague us tonight."

Perhaps made bold by these words, a fellow who was inside the house, the Sicilian lady's procurer, whom Andreuccio had neither seen nor heard, came to the window and in a loud, horrible, fierce voice said: "Who is down there?"

Andreuccio looked up when he heard the voice and saw a man who, from the little he could make out, looked as if he must be a brute of a fellow, with a thick black beard; and he kept yawning and rubbing his eyes as if he had just gotten out of bed or been awakened from a sound sleep. Not without fear, Andreuccio replied: "I am a brother of the lady inside."

But the fellow didn't let Andreuccio finish his reply; rather, in a much harsher tone than before, he said: "I don't know what's keeping me from going down there and caning you within an inch of your life — annoying, drunken ass that you are — for you are letting no one sleep tonight."

Several of the neighbors who knew the man well spoke kindly to Andreuccio: "By God, good man, go away, you don't want to get yourself killed tonight. Go, for your own good."

Andreuccio, frightened by the voice and the sight of the fellow, and urged by those who seemed to advise him out of a sense of charity, turned toward where he had followed the maidservant that day, without knowing where he was going, to return to his inn; but he was as sad as he could be, and disconsolate about his money. And since he couldn't stand the smell that was coming from him, he wanted to go to the sea to wash himself; so he turned left and started up a street called La Ruga Catalana. As he was heading toward the upper part of the city, he happened upon two men who were coming toward him with a lantern. Fearing that they might be the palace guard, or other men disposed to do evil, he hid in a shack that he saw nearby. But the two men, almost as if that was where they had been heading, also went into the same shack, where one of them, putting down some tools that he had been carrying on his shoulder, began to examine and discuss them with the other man.

While they were thus speaking, one of them said: "What does this mean? I smell the worst stench I ever smelled in my life." And holding up the lantern, they saw poor wretched Andreuccio, and asked in amazement: "Who's there?"

Andreuccio kept silent, but they came closer with the light and asked him what he was doing there all covered with filth. So Andreuccio told them everything that had happened to him. Realizing where this might have occurred, they said to themselves: "Truly, this fellow must have been in that scoundrel Buttafuoco's house."

And turning to him, one of them said: "Good man, even though you lost all your money, you have a great deal to thank God for, since chance had it that you fell and were unable to get back inside the house. For if you had not fallen, you can be sure that the moment you had fallen asleep you would have been murdered, and would have lost your life along with your money. But what good does it do to cry now? You have as much chance of getting your money back as you have of getting the stars from the sky. And you could very well end up dead, if that fellow hears that you've talked about what happened."

Having said this, they conferred with one another a little while, and said to him: "You see, we feel sorry for you; so, if you are willing to join us in something we are going to do, we are certain that you will end up with much more than you've lost." Andreuccio, who was desperate, replied that he was ready to go with them.

That day an archbishop of Naples, called Messire Filippo Minutolo, had been buried, with very rich decorations and a ruby on his finger worth more than five hundred gold florins. The men wanted to steal this ring, as they made known to Andreuccio.

Andreuccio, more greedy than wise, took off with them toward the cathedral; but he stunk so much that one of the men said: "Can't we find a way for this fellow to wash a little somewhere, so that he won't stink so awfully?" Said the other: "Yes, we're near a well where there is always a pulley and a big bucket; let's go there and we'll wash him in a trice."

When they arrived at the well, they found that the rope was there, but someone had taken the bucket. So they decided to tie the rope around Andreuccio and lower him into the well so he could wash himself, and when he had finished he would tug on the rope and they would haul him back up; so they lowered him down into the well.

While Andreuccio was down in the well, several of the palace guards came there because of the heat and because they were thirsty after having pursued someone and wanted a drink of water. Seeing them, the two robbers ran away before the palace guards could see them. Down at the bottom of the well, Andreuccio tugged the rope after he had finished washing himself. The guards, having laid down their shields, weapons, and doublets, began to pull up the rope, thinking that a bucket full of water was on the other end. As soon as Andreuccio saw he was at the rim of the well, he let go of the rope and jumped out. Seeing this, the palace guards were taken by surprise, and let go of the rope and began to run away as fast as they could. This amazed Andreuccio greatly, and if he hadn't been careful he might have fallen back into the well, injuring or even killing himself. But he got out and found the weapons, which he knew his two companions hadn't been carrying, and was even more astounded.

He was so confused, and so doleful about his bad fortune, that without touching anything he decided to leave that place, and took off toward he knew not where. As he was going along he encountered his two companions, who were coming back to pull him out of the well. Astounded, they asked him who had pulled him out. Andreuccio replied that he didn't know, and told them what had happened and what he had found outside the well. Realizing what must have happened, they laughingly told him why they had fled and who it had been that had pulled him out. Since it was already midnight, without saying anything further they went off to the cathedral. They got in quite easily and went up to the sarcophagus, which was made of marble and was very large. Using an iron bar, they lifted the lid, which was very heavy, far enough so that a man could get in, and propped it open. Then one of them began to say: "Who will get in?" To which the other replied: "Not I." "Nor I," said the first; "let Andreuccio get in." "That I will not do," said Andreuccio.

Turning on him, they both said: "What do you mean, you won't get in? In faith, if you don't get in, we'll hit you on the head with one of these iron bars until you drop dead."

Fearing for his life, Andreuccio climbed into the sarcophagus, thinking to himself: "They're making me get in to trick me; once I've handed them out everything, while I'm struggling to climb out, they'll take off and I'll be left with nothing." So he made up his mind to take his own share of the loot first of all; and remembering the precious ring that he had heard them speak about, as soon as he was inside the sarcophagus he removed the ring from the dead archbishop's finger and placed it on his own. Then he handed out the archbishop's pastoral staff, mitre, and gloves, and undressed him down to his shirt, handing them everything and saying that was all that was there. The two thieves knew that the ring should be there and told Andreuccio to look everywhere;

pretending to look for it, he kept them waiting a while and then replied that he couldn't find it. But they were as sly as he was; telling him to search for it again, they removed the bar that was propping up the lid of the sarcophagus and ran off, leaving Andreuccio trapped inside. Everyone can imagine what Andreuccio felt when he heard the lid slam shut.

He tried several times to lift the lid with his head and shoulders, but his efforts were in vain. So, defeated by great distress, he fainted away, falling on top of the dead body of the archbishop. Anyone who had seen them at that moment would have had a difficult time telling which one was dead, Andreuccio or the archbishop. But when he came to, he burst into tears, seeing that he must surely come to one of two ends: if no one came to open the sarcophagus, he must die there amid the stench and the worms of the dead body, or if someone did come and open the sarcophagus and found him there, he would be hanged for a thief.

Thinking these thoughts and suffering greatly, he heard the sound of many people moving about the church and speaking, and he realized that they had come there for the same reason that he and his companions had already done; and his fear grew far greater. But when they had opened the sarcophagus and propped the lid open, they began to argue about who should climb in, and none of them wished to do it. But after a long discussion a priest said: "What do you fear? Do you think he'll bite you? Dead men don't eat the living; I'll go in myself." And having said this, he leaned his chest against the rim of the sarcophagus and started to lower himself down feet first. Seeing this, Andreuccio rose up, and seizing the priest by one of his legs started to pull him down. When the priest felt this, he let out a loud scream and jumped back out of the sarcophagus. And he and all the others, frightened out of their wits, took off running as if they were being pursued by a hundred thousand devils, leaving the lid open.

Seeing this, Andreuccio, happy beyond what he had hoped, quickly jumped out and left the church by the way he had come in. It was almost daybreak, and with the ring on his finger he walked aimlessly until he came to the harbor, and then happened upon his inn, where he found that his travelling companions and the innkeeper had been worrying all night about what had happened to him. He recounted to them what had befallen him, and the innkeeper advised him to leave Naples immediately. He did so at once, returning to Perugia with his money invested in a ring, when he had gone to buy horses.'

Giovanni Boccaccio

Decameron DAY II, TALE 9

Bernabò of Genoa, duped by Ambrogiuolo, loses his wealth and orders that his innocent wife be put to death. She escapes and, disguised as a man, serves the Sultan. She finds the deceiver and brings Bernabò to Alexandria where, having punished the rogue, she once again puts on woman's garb. She and her husband return, wealthy once more, to Genoa.

Once Elissa had fulfilled her duty by telling her pitiful tale, the queen of the day,[1] Filomena, who was tall and lovely and had a surpassingly pleasant, smiling face, pulled herself up and said: 'We wish to keep our agreement with Dioneo, and since he and I are the only ones left who have not told a tale today, I shall tell mine first and he shall go last, as he requested.' Having said this, she began thus:

'There is a proverb, oft repeated, to the effect that the deceiver

---

1. In the "frame story" of the *Decameron*, a group of young people who have fled the plague in Florence and taken refuge in the countryside pass the time by each telling a story about a particular theme for a period of ten days. Each day has a "king" or "queen" who selects the theme for the tales told that day.

remains at the feet of the deceived. This does not seem to be proved true by any reason, but is shown by events that occur. Thus, dear ladies, following the theme of the day, it occurred to me to show you that this is indeed true. Nor should it displease you to have heard it, so that you will know how to protect yourselves from deceivers.

Several important Italian merchants were staying at an inn in Paris, for one reason or other, as they were accustomed to do. One evening after a convivial meal together, they began to speak about diverse matters, and passing from one subject to another they came to speak about their wives, whom they had left at home.

One began in a bantering tone to say, "I know not what my wife does, but I do know that when I encounter some young woman here whom I fancy, I put aside the love I bear toward my wife and take from the one here whatever pleasure I can."

Another replied: "I do likewise, for whether I believe she does or not, my wife can have her own adventures; so it's tit for tat. What's sauce for the goose is sauce for the gander."

A third man spoke in almost the same terms. In short, they all seemed to be in agreement that the women whom they left behind all took advantage of the situation.

Only one, a man from Genoa named Bernabò Lomellin, said the opposite, stating that by the special grace of God, he had a wife who was endowed with all the virtues and talents that a lady or even a gentleman or a page in a princely household should have, and that perhaps in all of Italy there was not another woman such as she; for she was lovely looking and still quite young, graceful, and attractive; and there was nothing that a woman could do, such as fancy work in silk and such things, that she didn't do better than any other woman. Besides this, Bernabò said that there was no equerry or steward who could serve better or more scrupulously at a gentleman's table than she did, for she was extremely well bred, wise, and discreet. He also stated that she could ride, hawk, read and write, and do accounts better than if she were a merchant. Thence, after much more praise, he came to the subject of which they had been speaking, and said that he could swear that there was no woman more honest or chaste than she;

for which reason he believed that if he stayed away from home for ten years, or even forever, she would never have an adventure with another man.

Among the group at the inn was a young merchant from Piacenza called Ambrogiuolo, who laughed fit to burst about this last bit of praise from Bernabò about his lady. And, mocking Bernabò, Ambrogiuolo asked him if the emperor had granted him a privilege that had been granted to no other man. Somewhat troubled, Bernabò answered that this privilege had been granted to him not by the emperor but by God, who had a little more power than the emperor.

Then Ambrogiuolo said: "Bernabò, I have no doubt that you believe you are speaking the truth, but it seems to me that you haven't reflected on the nature of things; for if you had, I do not hold you to be of such an inferior intellect that you would not have recognized things in Nature that would make you speak more rationally about this matter. And so you won't think that we who have spoken so loosely about our wives believe that ours are different, or differently made, than yours, but rather that we have spoken out of a natural awareness, I wish to discourse a little with you about this matter. I have always heard that of all the mortal animals created by God, man is the noblest, and woman the next. But man, as is generally believed and seen in his actions, is more perfect than woman. And since man has more perfection, without fail he must have more constancy — and so he does, for women are universally more fickle. This could be demonstrated by many natural reasons, which for the present I shall not go into. But if man is of greater constancy, and he cannot restrain himself from desiring a woman whom he finds attractive — much less from giving in to a woman who entices him — and, beyond mere desire, he does whatever he can to be with her, and this occurs not once a month but a thousand times a day; how can you expect a woman, who is inconstant by nature, to resist the entreaties, flattery, gifts, and the thousand other wiles that a clever man who desires her will use? As much as you say that your wife is faithful, I don't think you really believe it. You yourself say that she is made of flesh and blood like other women. If that is so, she must have the same desires and the same powers as other women to resist their natural appetites. So, as honest as she may be, she still may very well do as other women do, and nothing that is possible can be so vehemently denied, or stated to the contrary, as you do."

Bernabò replied: "I am a merchant and not a philosopher, and I shall answer as a merchant. I know that what you say can happen to foolish women who have no shame. But women who are wise are so solicitous of their honor that they become stronger than men, who from what I can see care nothing for their honor. My wife is one such woman."

Ambrogiuolo said: "Truly, if every time they committed an indiscretion, women grew a horn on their forehead as evidence of what they had done, I believe that few would indulge in them. But it seems that clever women don't grow horns, nor do they leave any footprints or other evidence; and shame and loss of honor consist only in evident things. So, when they can do so secretly, they do; or if they are foolish, they don't. Know this for certain: the only chaste women are those who have never been courted by any man, or, if they themselves have pursued a man, they were not satisfied. And as much as I know these to be natural, true reasons, I would not speak at such length of these things if I had not proven them to be so, many times and with many women. I tell you, if I were around that saintly wife of yours, I believe that I would lead her to do what I have led others to do, in a short space of time."

Disturbed by this, Bernabò replied: "Debating with words can go on too long; you would say one thing and I another, and in the end it would amount to nothing. But since you say that all woman are so tractable, and that you are so clever, to convince you of my wife's honesty, I am willing to have my head chopped off if you should ever succeed in inducing her to give in to you in such an act; and if you fail, I wish you to lose nothing more than a thousand gold florins."

Ambrogiuolo, excited by the argument, replied: "Bernabò, I know not what I would do with your head, if I won. But if you wish to see proof of what I have said, wager against my thousand florins, five thousand gold florins of your own, which should be less dear to you than your head. Moreover, whereas you place no time limit on the wager, I wish to oblige myself to go to Genoa, and within three months from the day I leave Paris, I shall have had my way with your wife. As a sign of this I shall bring back with me some of the things that are dearest to her, and so many and such signs that you yourself shall admit that it is true. But I do so on the condition that you promise me by your faith that you will neither go to Genoa nor write anything of this matter to her during that time."

Bernabò said that he was well pleased with the wager; and even though the other merchants who were there endeavored to prevent this, realizing that great evil could come of it, the spirits of the two men were so inflamed that, against the wishes of all the others, they pledged themselves to one another in documents written in their own hand.

Having thus pledged, Bernabò remained in Paris and Ambrogiuolo left for Genoa as soon as he could. After staying there for several days and very discreetly finding out where the lady lived and what her habits were, he learned all that, and more than he had heard from Bernabò — which led him to believe that he had been mad to make such a wager. But he came to an understanding with a poor woman who went frequently to Bernabò's house and of whom his wife was very fond. Ambrogiuolo could not succeed in getting the woman to do anything else, so he bribed her into smuggling him not only into the gentle lady's house, but into her bedchamber, in a chest that he had had specially made. Acting upon Ambrogiuolo's orders, the good woman pretended that she had to go off somewhere, and asked if she could leave the chest there for a few days.

So the chest remained in the lady's bedchamber. When nighttime came, as soon as Ambrogiuolo could tell that she was asleep, he used a special device that he had had made to open the chest. He crept out and into the bedchamber, where a light was burning. He began to regard the arrangement of the room, the paintings, and everything else of note that was there, and to fix them in his memory. Then he approached the bed, and discerning that the lady and a little girl who was with her were fast asleep, he gently lifted the covers until she was completely revealed, and saw that she was as lovely naked as she was clothed. He could see no distinguishing mark on her except a mole under her left breast, around which were several fine golden hairs. Having seen these, he quietly covered her up again, although, seeing how lovely she was, he was tempted to put his own life in danger and lie down beside her. But having heard how harsh and cold[2] she was about such things, he did not risk it. Ambrogiuolo spent most of the night at his leisure in the bedchamber, and took a purse and a cloak out of a strong box of hers, as well as several rings and belts, put it all into the chest, climbed back in, and closed the lid as before; and in this way he passed two nights without the lady realizing anything. On the third day, according to plan, the good woman returned for her chest and took it away. Ambrogiuolo emerged and paid off the woman as promised, and returned to Paris with the things as soon as possible, before the agreed-upon time had elapsed.

There he called together Bernabò and the merchants who had been present during the discussion and the wager, and said that he had won the wager because he had brought back what he had boasted he would. And to prove that this was true, first he described the room and the paintings in it, and then he showed the things of hers that he had brought back, declaring that she had given them to him. Bernabò admitted that the room was as he described it and that he recognized the things as belonging to his wife; but he said that Ambrogiuolo could have learned about the room from one of the servants in the house, and could have obtained the things in the same way. So if Ambrogiuolo had nothing else to say, it did not seem to Bernabò that this was enough to win the wager.

So Ambrogiuolo said: "Truly, this should have sufficed; but since you want me to say more, I shall do so. I tell you that your wife Madonna Ginevra has under her left breast a fairly large mole with about six golden hairs around it."

When Bernabò heard this, he looked as if he had been stabbed in the heart, he was so distressed; and, with a totally altered visage, though he hadn't said a word, he gave a very clear sign that what Ambrogiuolo was saying was true. After a while he said: "Sirs, what Ambrogiuolo says is true; so, since he has won the wager, let him come whenever he wants and he shall be paid." And, thus, the next day Ambrogiuolo was paid in full.

Bernabò left Paris with evil in his heart toward his wife, and headed toward Genoa. As he approached the city, he didn't enter, but remained about twenty miles away, on an estate of his. He sent one of his servants, in whom he had great trust, with two horses and a letter to Genoa, telling the lady that he had returned and that she should come to him with the servant. And secretly he ordered the servant, as soon as he was in some place that seemed best to him, to kill the woman with no mercy and then to return to him. When the servant arrived in Genoa and delivered the letter and the message, he was joyfully received by the lady. The following day she rode off with him toward their estate.

Riding along and discoursing of various things, they came to a very deep, lonely valley surrounded by high grottoes and trees; the servant, feeling this to be a safe place to carry out his master's order, drew out a knife and took the lady by the arm, saying: "My lady, commend your soul to God, for you must die here."

Seeing the knife and hearing these words, the lady, terribly frightened, said: "For the love of God, before you slay me, tell me how I have offended you that you should want to kill me."

"My lady," said the servant, "you have not offended me in any way. I know not how you have offended your husband, but he has ordered me to slay you on this road and to show no mercy, and he threatened to have me hanged by the neck if I did not do it. You know very well how attached to him I am and that I cannot say no to anything he orders me to do. God knows, I am sorry for you, but I cannot do otherwise."

Weeping, the lady replied: "Alas! Have mercy, for the love of God! Do not become the murderer of one who never hurt you in order to serve your master. God, who knows everything, knows that I never did anything for which my husband should reward me in this way. But let us leave that now; if you wish, you can please God and your master and me at the same time: take these garments of mine and give me just your doublet and a hood, and return to your master and mine and say that you have slain me. I swear to you, by the life you will have given me, that I shall go far away to a place whence no news of me shall come either to him or to you."

The servant, who was loath to slay Madonna Ginevra, readily took pity on her. So he took her garments and gave her a little doublet and a hood and left her with the money she had, praying her to go far away from there and leaving her on foot in the valley. He returned to his master, to whom he said that not only had his orders been carried out, but that he had left her body to the wolves. After some time Bernabò returned to Genoa, and when the story came to be known, he was strongly censured.

The lady, left alone and disconsolate, waited until nightfall and then, disguised as best as she could, walked to a nearby village, where she procured what she needed from an old woman. She had the doublet fitted to her, shortened it, had her shift made into a pair of short breeches, cut her hair short, and totally transformed herself to look like a sailor. She headed toward the sea, where by chance at Alba she met a kind man from Catalonia whose name was Signor En Cararh, who had come on land from a ship of his, which was anchored at some distance from there, to refresh himself at a fountain. She entered into conversation with him, signed on as his servant, and boarded the ship, calling herself Sicurano da Finale. There, dressed in better clothes like a gentleman, Sicurano began to serve the Catalonian so well and so obligingly that he prized him above everything. After a short time, this Catalonian sailed with a shipload to Alexandria, bringing some peregrine falcons to the Sultan. The Sultan had him to dine several times, and observing the manners of Sicurano, who always came along to serve his master, and being greatly pleased, he asked the Catalonian to leave him in Alexandria. As loath as he was to do so, the Catalonian left Sicurano with the Sultan.

In a short time, Sicurano won the favor and love of the Sultan with his handsome ways, as he had done with the Catalonian. The time of year came when a fair brought a great number of Christian and Saracen merchants to Acri, which was under the Sultan's sovereignty. Now the Sultan always used to send several of his courtiers in addition to other officers to guard the merchants and their wares. That year, he decided to send Sicurano, who already knew the language very well.

Thus Sicurano came to Acri as captain of the guard, solicitously performing the duties that appertained to his office. As he went on his rounds he saw many merchants — Sicilians, Pisans, Genoese, Venetians, and other Italians — and he was glad to mingle with them in memory of his homeland. Now it happened that on one occasion when Sicurano had dismounted at the warehouse of some Venetian merchants, he caught sight of a purse and a belt that he immediately recognized as having been his own, and was astonished. But without letting on, he graciously asked to whom they belonged, and whether that person would like to sell them.

Ambrogiuolo had come to Acri from Piacenza on a Venetian ship with a great deal of merchandise. Hearing that the captain of the guard was asking to whom these things belonged, he came forward and laughingly said: "Sire, the things are mine, and I will not sell them; but if you like them, I shall gladly give them to you."

Seeing Ambrogiuolo laugh, Sicurano suspected that he had somehow recognized him. But putting on a brave face, he said: "Perhaps you laugh to see me, a man of arms, asking about these feminine things."

Said Ambrogiuolo: "Sire, I don't laugh at that; I am thinking of how I gained them."

To which Sicurano said: "Go to! May God give you good fortune. If it is not unseemly, tell us how you gained them."

"Sire," said Ambrogiuolo, "these things were given to me, with some other items, by a gentle lady of Genoa called Madonna Ginevra, the wife of Bernabò Lomellin, one night when I lay with her; she begged me to keep them for love of her. I laughed just now because I was reminded of the foolishness of Bernabò, who was mad enough to wager five thousand gold florins against a thousand that I would not have my way with his lady, which I did, and won the prize. Bernabò, who should have punished himself for his own idiocy rather than her for doing what all women do, returned from Paris to Genoa and, from what I later heard, had her slain."

Hearing this, Sicurano immediately understood what had been the reason for Bernabò's rage, and clearly recognized Ambrogiuolo as the cause of all his troubles. And he decided that he could not let him go unpunished. So, Sicurano acted as though he liked the story very well, and carefully set about making friends with Ambrogiuolo, to the point that when the fair was over, Ambrogiuolo returned with Sicurano to Alexandria, where Sicurano had a warehouse built for him and put a great deal of money into his hands. Seeing how advantageous it was for him there, Ambrogiuolo was happy to remain in Alexandria. Sicurano, who was anxious to let Bernabò know of his innocence, did not rest until he got some important Genoese merchants who were in Alexandria to give Bernabò a reason to come there. Sicurano saw to it that Bernabò, who was reduced to a state of great poverty, was taken in by one of Sicurano's friends. Then Sicurano waited until he thought it was the right time to carry out his plans.

Sicurano had already had Ambrogiuolo tell his story before the Sultan, who enjoyed it a great deal. But when he saw that Bernabò was there, thinking that it was no time to delay, he waited for the right moment and saw to it that Ambrogiuolo and Bernabò were both called before the Sultan. He had determined that if it could not be done gently, then the truth about what Ambrogiuolo was boasting about Bernabò's wife should be gotten out of him by force. When Ambrogiuolo and Bernabò had come, with a severe look on his face, the Sultan asked Ambrogiuolo in the presence of many people to tell the truth about how he had won the five thousand gold florins from Bernabò. Sicurano, in whom Ambrogiuolo had the greatest trust, was also there, and with an exceedingly angry face threatened Ambrogiuolo with grave tortures if he did not tell the truth. So

Ambrogiuolo, frightened on all sides, yet still rather hesitantly, told the whole story in front of Bernabò and many others, expecting no other punishment save that of having to return the five thousand gold florins.

When Ambrogiuolo had spoken, Sicurano, acting as the Sultan's executor, turned to Bernabò and said: "And what did you do about this lie about your wife?"

Bernabò replied: "Vanquished by rage at the loss of my money and the shame I thought had been brought upon me by my wife, I had her slain by one of my servants. And according to what he reported to me, she was immediately devoured by a pack of wolves."

These things were all said in the presence of the Sultan, who did not yet know what Sicurano, who had arranged all this, was trying to achieve. Sicurano said to him: "My Lord, you can clearly see how that good woman can glory in both her lover and her husband: for her lover deprived her of her honor through lies, ruining her reputation, and impoverishing her husband at the same time; and her husband, more willing to believe another man's lies than the truth of which he had such a long experience, had her slain and devoured by wolves. And beyond that, the love that her lover and her husband bear her is so great that neither one of them recognizes her, though they have been in her presence for some time. But in order that you might fully know what each of them has deserved, if you will grant me the special favor of both punishing the deceiver and pardoning the deceived, I shall have her come here into your presence and theirs."

The Sultan, who was disposed to please Sicurano in everything he wished in this matter, said that it pleased him to grant his request, and told him to have the woman brought before him. Bernabò, who firmly believed her to be dead, was astounded. Ambrogiuolo, who could already guess the evil that was about to befall him, feared that he would have a worse punishment than paying back the money; nor did he know what to hope for or to fear if the woman should appear. Bewildered, he awaited her arrival.

The Sultan having granted Sicurano's request, Sicurano burst into tears and threw himself at the Sultan's feet, seeming at one and the same time to leave off speaking in a man's voice and acting like a man, and said: "My Lord, I am the wretched, unfortunate Ginevra, who has gone wandering around the world for six years disguised as a man, falsely and evilly slandered by this traitor Ambrogiuolo, and given over by this unjust man to be slain by one of his servants and devoured by wolves." And tearing open the front of her garments she revealed her breast, showing the Sultan and everyone else there that she was a woman. She then turned angrily to Ambrogiuolo and asked him when he had ever lain with her, as he had boasted. Ambrogiuiolo, recognizing her and rendered almost mute by shame, said nothing.

The Sultan, who had always thought that Sicurano was a man, was so amazed that at several points he believed that what he was seeing and hearing was a dream rather than reality. But when his amazement abated and he learned the truth, he commended the life and constancy of Ginevra, who up to that time had been called Sicurano, with the greatest praise. He ordered that she be brought the noblest feminine garments and ladies-in-waiting, and at her request pardoned Bernabò from the death he deserved. When Bernabò recognized her, he threw himself at her feet, weeping, and asked forgiveness. Unworthy as he was, she benevolently forgave him, lifting him to his feet and tenderly embracing him as her husband.

Shortly afterward the Sultan ordered that Ambrogiuolo be tied to a stake in some elevated place in the city, in the sun, with honey smeared all over him, and that he not be released; and it was done. After this he ordered that what had belonged to Ambrogiuolo be given to the lady; this was more than ten thousand doubloons. Then he had a beautiful celebration prepared, and honored Bernarbò as the husband of Madonna Ginevra and Madonna Ginevra as the most valorous of women. And he gave them jewels and gold and silver plate and money, for a value of more than ten thousand doubloons more. He saw to it that a ship was placed at their disposal, and after the celebration he gave them leave to return to Genoa when they pleased. They returned thence very wealthy and with great joy, and were received with the greatest honor — especially Madonna Ginevra, who everyone had thought was dead. And as long as she lived she was always held to be a lady of great virtue and eminence.

Ambrogiuolo, tied to the stake and smeared with honey, was tormented with the greatest agony by flies and wasps and horseflies, in which that country abounds. Not only did he die; his flesh was eaten down to the bones, which were left white, held together by the tendons. For a long time his bones remained there as a testimony of his wickedness for whoever saw them. Thus the deceiver was left at the feet of the deceived.'

Giovanni Boccaccio

LETTER TO FRANCESCO NELLI

A Merchant with Political Power and Royal Pretensions

Niccola or Niccolò Acciaiuoli (1310–1365), a member of the Florentine family of merchants that also operated in Naples (where Niccola was sent in 1331), was one of the leading men on the commercial scene and one of the shrewdest, most powerful politicians in Italy during the mid-fourteenth century. He became increasingly powerful after 1335 (especially during the long reign of Queen Joanna I of Naples.) He was Great Seneschal and one of the dominant figures of the Angevin dynasty; his influence was felt in Greece, Avignon, at the Byzantine court and the Papal curia. But his imperious, haughty character, his vanity, and his mania for power and recognition (even literary recognition, which he expected from no less than Petrarch) made him an object of diffidence and even scorn. In a famous letter to Francesco Nelli, Giovanni Boccaccio, who had been Acciaiuoli's comrade in the merchant trade and had shared with him the joyous social life of Naples when both men had been in that city in their twenties, between about 1130 and 1138, paints a merciless portrait of Niccola as an arrogant, egomaniacal politician.[1] *The two men had been so close that Boccaccio wrote*

---

1. For more on the relationship between Acciaiuoli and Boccaccio see my *Boccaccio: The Man and His Works*, 1976.

Acciaiuoli several letters, and dedicated his "De mulieribus claris" to Niccolò's sister, Andrea Acciaiuoli. But Boccaccio was always disappointed in his hope that Acciaiuoli would obtain for him a position at the court of Naples like the one that had been offered to Petrarch and then assigned to the mediocre poet Zanobi da Strada, a friend of both Acciauoli and Boccaccio.

The following passage is from Boccaccio's Letter XIII and was written after a particularly disappointing stay in Acciaiuoli's home when he was at the height of his power (between November 1362 and March 1363). It paints a Rabelaisian portrait of the enterprising merchant who had successfully scaled the heights of political power but had remained fundamentally vulgar and pretentious; indeed, he had become an object of ridicule on account of his vanity and the royal airs he affected.

I had thought that, having risen so high, he would change his old ways for the better. But as I clearly realized, success has made him worse. First of all, he has no care or benevolence toward the miserable wretches who serve him; it's all wasted breath. Let it rain, hail, or even snow, let the winds make the world tumble down, let thunder frighten mortal men, lightning threaten fire and death, rivers overflow their banks, robbers plague the highways, horses break down from exhaustion; as many horrible things might happen inside the house or out, he still will not be moved by pity for the miserable creatures who serve him. He will help them neither with advice, nor words, nor actions, as if they were Arabs or Indians or wild beasts. As long as he himself is all right, everyone else can suffer as much as they like. I think that he believes that it's part of his greatness to tread upon and despise those who are lower than he; and a sign of even greater cruelty is the fact that if he sees or hears that his friends are ill, he does not help them as friends usually do, or at least comfort them with words; rather, he does not wish to hear about his friends who are in need. If it were up to him, they would die like animals without any doctor's advice or even the last sacraments. Who wouldn't be horrified at this inhuman behavior? Who would not fear it? Is there no cruelty so barbarous that friendship does not honor it with some pity? We read the examples of great men in vain — indeed, to our detriment — if we act in the opposite manner. This is not what is taught by Valerius Maximus, with whom your Patron so often says he is very familiar. He should remember Marcus Marcellus, who wept for the misfortunes of the Syracusans,[2] and learn from this. For if illustrious men weep for their enemies, think what must be due their friends. Similarly, he should recall to mind the praiseworthy action of Alexander, King of Macedonia, when it was freezing cold and the conqueror of Asia saw fit to descend from his throne near the fire, and place upon it with his own hands one of the most humble, oldest soldiers who was suffering greatly from the excessive cold, so that he might feel the comfort of the fire.[3] Surely the spirits of friends are heartened, and those of enemies are humbled, by clemency in faith and service, while incivility and negligence alienate the hearts of friends.

In addition to this, he says he has found laws, I know not whether in Phoroneus[4] or Licurgus[5] or Cato,[6] according to which if anyone in his retinue should die, any will or testament that might exist is ignored, and he himself becomes the sole heir; even creditors, if there are any, are ignored. He pretends that the dead man owes him a great deal, even though he himself might owe money to the defunct. How appalled I was at these unknown laws of his from Appius[7] or Cato or Lelius[8] or Ulpianus![9]

He does another very unkind, disturbing thing which, although

---

2. Valerius Maximus V, I, 4.

3. Valerius Maximus V, XI.

4. The progenitor of the Argives (inhabitants of Argos, and, by extension, the ancient Greeks). According to tradition, Phoroneus was the first to teach men how to use fire and to gather together in social communities.

5. A legislator to whom the Spartans attributed their legal system.

6. The famous Roman censor Marcus Portius Cato (234-149 B.C.).

7. Appius Claudius Caecus (ca.340–ca.273 B.C.), a Roman consul known as a political reformer and writer on legal matters. He organized the construction of the first paved Roman road, the Via Appia.

8. Gaius Lelius, a Roman of the mid-second century B.C.; one of the interlocutors in Cicero's *Cato Maior*.

9. Domitius Ulpianus, a celebrated Roman jurisconsult who died in 228 A.D.

everyone knows about it, I would not reveal to anyone but you; but because you are a friend and you know everything about him, I shall faithfully tell it to you as proof of what I'm saying about him. He frequently goes into his inner sanctum and, so that it will seem that he has a great deal of important business for the crown, he has men placed at the doors, the way the royal family does, and no one who asks permission to enter is allowed to do so. Many come, and sometimes very highly placed men; they fill the courtyard in front of the door and in a low voice ask for permission to speak to him. The answers given by the men guarding the doors are laughable. To many they reply that he is in conference; to others, that he is saying the divine office; to others, that he is resting after his great toils over state affairs, and so on. And in the end he does nothing except what it is said of Caesar Domitian,[10] who would spend hours catching flies and stabbing them with a stylus.[11] Although I am not one of his entourage and have no desire to be, nevertheless I know what goes on in his chambers. He orders that a chair be placed in his dressing room, just like her majesty's throne, and there he sits surrounded by his women, who are not whores, for that would be too unseemly, nor sisters nor relatives nor nieces, and amid discordant noises from his belly he expels the stinking load from his guts while great councils are held and the affairs of the Kingdom of Naples are dealt with; prefectures are appointed, oral reports are given, and letters to the kings of the world and to the supreme pontiff and to other friends are dictated and written and corrected, with all the flatterers and Greeks and women standing around nodding their approval. And the fools who are waiting in the courtyard believe that he, received into the council room of the gods, is holding solemn council with them about the general state of the republic. Oh, great patience of God! What shall you say to this? With the tedium of long waiting, he slays those whom he

---

10. Titus Flavius Domitianus (A.D. 51–96), Roman emperor from 81 to 96 A.D.
11. Suetonius, *The Lives of the Caesars*, Book VIII, *Domitian*, 3, I. Domitian ruled Rome from 86 to 91 A.D., and began the second wave of persecutions of the Christians.

could have satisfied with a few words or with his presence. I recall how many times and how much more easily I have been able to obtain leave to speak with the supreme pontiff and with the Emperor Charles[12] and many other great princes than many very noble men, not to mention the others, have been able to do with this man while he sits relieving himself. There is no doubt that he incurs the hatred of many, while he could have earned their grace; for while he believes, like the ancient king of Persia,[13] that by withholding himself from the eyes of his friends or those who need him, he is enhancing the majesty of his name, in reality he is earning the indignation of many; and the indignation of the people can harm even the greatest kings. Nor is it wise to believe that he is deceiving those who are forced to wait with this disgusting way he has of hiding. Even the lowly sometimes see, with the eyes of a lynx, what goes on within the chambers of men such as he. But finally, after he has for a long time made sport of those who are asking for him, and has even bored himself, the doors open and he emerges in public with his forehead furrowed as if he had many serious matters on his mind, sighing, and looks about him. The poor wretches who are waiting turn to him as he comes out, and with meek voices suffocated by tears and sadness ask to be heard; but he, acting as if he were preoccupied by very grave thoughts, pretends not to hear what is said to him if he doesn't want to. And although he sometimes replies, all he really does is put off the wretches with empty promises and twisted words. Why am I saying all this? He treats everyone as if he were the only one infused with a soul from heaven, while all the others were brute beasts. Miserable me! I cannot restrain my pen from taking me where I would wish not to go. Has this man so forgotten what he was like before, when he came as a merchant to Naples and was happy to have just one servant? And that was not in the distant times when Ascanius or rather Silvius was

---

12. Charles IV, who ruled the Holy Roman Empire from 1347 to 1378; Boccaccio may have been received by him in 1355.
13. Marcus Junianus Justinus, I, 9, 12.

founding Alba;[14] it wasn't even thirty years ago. There are still many people alive who remember, and I am one of them. Whence comes this great pride, whence this intolerable disdain for everyone? His is not the race of the great Jove, nor the wealth of Darius, nor the strength of Hercules, nor the wisdom of Solomon. Surely he is great no less on account of the misfortunes of men greater than he than on account of his own merit; when good men fall, bad ones often rise up to take their places. But let us concede that he got to where good fortune has brought him by his own talents, and let us also add, if you wish, the preeminence of each great king. Should he thus mistreat those who are not as great as he? Fortune is fickle; she knocks to the ground those whom she has raised up, nor does she ever leave anything in the same state under the sun. Doesn't this Patron of yours remember reading about King Xerxes of Persia,[15] who blanketed the earth with soldiers and the seas with ships to wage war against the Greeks, and when they had routed him and his armies were torn apart and driven out and worn out by pestilence and his fleet destroyed, he had to humbly beg some fishermen near the Hellespont to take him back to Asia from Europe?

---

14. Alba Longa was both neighbor and rival to Rome. According to tradition, the town was founded by Ascanius, son of the Trojan hero Aeneas. In other accounts, it is Silvius, Ascanius' son, who founds Alba Longa.

15. Xerxes, son of Darius, is a classic example of pride that is punished; see Dante, *Purgatory* XXVIII, 71 ff.

Domenico Lenzi il Biadaiolo

MIRROR OF HUMANITY

Siena the Perverse Acts Against the Poor
During the Famine of 1339

How there was a great famine in Florence and in other parts of the world, and how the Sienese expelled all the poor people from their city, and the Florentines received them.

Such a cruel famine and shortage of food went on here in Florence,[1] that you who read this account surely must know that other parts of the world were affected as well. According to reliable eyewitnesses, it was felt so cruelly and harshly that the poor had nothing to eat but plant roots and fruits of trees, and meats disgusting not only to the mouth, but to the nose as well. Italy, and especially Tuscany, was more overwhelmed by this pestilence than any other place. But I can say that during this time of famine my fatherland, Florence — whose countryside does not produce enough grain to support it for 5 months, and where victuals

---

1. From 1328 to 1330. The uprising described below erupted in Siena in April 1329 (not May, as Lenzi writes). It appears that Lenzi was writing about these events at a distance of several years, based on what he himself remembered or had recorded, and with unrelenting animosity toward the city of Siena.

are always more expensive than in any other part of Italy — by itself supported half of the poor of Tuscany through the providence and aid of the good wealthy people and their money.² Thus it might be said, and indeed is true, that the poor, having been expelled from the grain-rich surrounding lands for fear they might seize them, and having been deprived of the remedies offered to assist them, could only turn to Florence as a trusted port of consolation. During the aforementioned famine Florence not once but many times graciously sustained the poor and others, each in his own degree.

Now, I certainly would prefer to remain silent about such events as now occur to my mind; but I cannot suffer that such cruel insolence and miscarriage of mercy as that which the decadent, perverse, cruel, insane Siena showed during this famine should go untold. For Siena was so insolent and presumptuous as to blindly act against the disinherited poor when they were all cruelly bereft of benevolent mercy, giving full rein to her impious cruelty. Would that those perfidious citizens of the city of the she-wolf³ had not been borne and suckled by their mother, who not only devours flesh, but swallows up even the earth, and viciously assails the winds with all her cruel forces.

But, sirs, I know not whether to prove they are made of different stuff, or to bring down greater and more cruel judgment of their evils by Him who is the height of compassion, at first there had been someone in Siena, the minister of the Hospice of Santa Maria della Scala,⁴ who was willing to give so many alms to the poor that it seemed that all of God's power were intervening. To everyone — women, men, children and adults — was given a loaf of bread weighing 14 *once*;⁵ if a woman was with child, she was given two loaves. Such great and open charity attracted the

---

2. Probably an allusion to the *prestanze* (forced or voluntary loans) to which the Florentine government had recourse during times of sudden necessity.

3. A symbol of Siena, and also the name of one of the city's *contrade* or districts.

4. Giovanni di Tese dei Tolomei was rector of the Hospice of Santa Maria della Scala from 1314 to 1339.

5. An *oncia* was equivalent to a little less than 30 grams.

poor, who came from near and far. But the alms did not run out even though the number of hungry people increased, for a way was found to replenish them by having everyone contribute to such a good cause. Thus, as can be seen in the painting on the next pages,[6] this was how it was organized: alms were distributed three days of the week — that is, Monday, Wednesday, and Friday — to as many poor as came to the Hospice of la Scala for that reason. All of the poor people would enter, and then three doors were left open through which they left the building; one was for men, the other was used by the women, and the third was for little children, who streamed out continuously. At each of the doors were positioned two very worthy members of the Hospice, who distributed the alms to the people as they emerged.

Oh! Great God, You should grant Your grace directly to that house! But we know that only from You, O Lord, does good proceed, and that whoever out of love for You imparts his goods to Your ambassadors the poor, by Your virtue and power that good will abound in his house without discord.

But, dear readers, regard this "Mirror" entitled "Mirror of Humanity," which recounts such godless behavior, heeding God who gave Himself to so much goodness. The city of Siena became envious, and in her insane iniquity clandestinely opposed what Messire Giovanni was doing. The Council of Nine[7] sent for Messire Giovanni; when he came into their presence, he asked what they wished of him. O prideful Siena, let the whole world hear what you are! They replied that under pain of death by fire this almsgiving should not continue thenceforward. Take heed, all men! These people were not only ordering that an injury be done to God; but that all those to whom only God is a brother should be allowed to die of hunger, in a prosperous city that had plenty of food. For I say, sirs, that these men were well brought up and trained by their mother the she-wolf; let this argument alone be brought against them, without any other syllogisms.

---

6. There is no miniature corresponding to this passage in the original codex, either because it was never painted or inserted, or was later removed.

7. The highest magistrates of Siena.

But even if this helps no one else, listen to how this evil went forward; now I shall recount how they went on. Having given this grim order, that city continued thus:

The next day the poor returned to the Hospice, their accustomed refuge, believing that they would receive the usual charity and relief, and that when they heard the word "Enter," they would all be comforted. But that sweet greeting became an ill-fortuned dismissal, for this is what they heard instead: "Go away, you hungry beggars, to perish along with your wants, for the lords of this city have ordered that you be left to perish in your misery; otherwise both we and our houses and possessions will be consumed by fire. We have no more charity in us." At this cruel, arrogant reply, there arose infinite cries and sounds of hands striking, shouts and crying, and people clawing their faces so deeply that they seemed to bear the marks of nails. Throughout the entire city, countryside, castles, and fortresses could be heard the voices of people crying for someone in their family who had died. And thus the poor ran desperately in infinite numbers toward the public palace whence those orders had emanated, crying out "Have mercy!" or "Fire!" or "Die!" All this noise brought the people of the city running, armed with whatever they could find. Armed guards emerged from the public palace to put down the uprising, but to little avail; for the poor, striking with stones and sticks, stormed the palace, driving back the guards, who were fearful of greater injury.

At this Guido Ricci da Reggio,[8] the captain of the army of that city, came running into the fray. One of the guards, carrying a staff and caring nothing for death, came up and struck him a blow on the lower back, knocking him off his feet; and if it hadn't been for the strong armor he was wearing, he might have died. There was great confusion, and many on all sides were gravely wounded. If it hadn't been that God did not wish it, that day Siena might have been properly paid back for her thieving, evil ways, providing a fearful reminder for all ages.

---

8. Guidoriccio da Fogliano, the *condottiere* depicted by Simone Martini in a famous fresco (1328) in the public palace at Siena.

Domenico Lenzi il Biadaiolo

Several days after the uprising had quieted down, there began an intense search for whoever had incited or consented to so much violence and turmoil. In one night, no fewer than 60 men were taken from their beds, and as many were tortured as were hanged by the neck, including the man who had felled the captain. And there may have been men among those who were hanged who had never even heard about the uprising. More than a hundred men were exiled at that time; but that's the way that city is! The others remained in prison for several days.

But this did not end the cruel assaults of fiery Siena; for at a public council it was voted that the poor should be driven out of Siena and that no further succor for the love of God was to be given them.

Oh! Cruel earth, why did you not open up?[9]

There came the blare of a trumpet and then a human voice declared that under pain of death, every poor stranger should leave the city within three days' time. Police squadrons went around with clubs and stones, cruelly driving people out of the city gates, caring not if they were children or adults, women or men, with child or not. Those who had been driven out of Siena turned to Florence as their certain source of relief and mercy; they were well received and well treated there. And giving thanks to God, they devoutly prayed that He would keep Florence in His blessed peace and that she and her citizens be worthily praised . . .

---

9. A quotation from Dante's *Inferno* (XXXIII, 66), powerfully dramatic in its allusion to the desperate plight of Count Ugolino and his sons and grandsons.

Messire Villano Tortures Merchants Suspected of Hoarding Grain

When the Council of Six called the grain merchants before them in September 1329.

On the 18th of this month, the Grain Council called before them 60 men, grain and feed merchants. They quickly appeared before the Six, saying: "We are all here at your request. What do you command of us?" The Six conferred together and said: "We cannot be with you nor confer with you now, for there is no time; but, in brief, we would like to ask your advice on whether there is any way to get the price of grain to come down. We know you will give us good advice, with the help of God, since you know all about these things. Go now, and return early tomorrow and we shall see to it that our officer Messire Villano[10] meets with you; and we pray you to confer well with him and to advise him on what you think is the best course to take." Then they were given leave to go.

The next day, that is, Tuesday morning, they all gathered in the square of Orsanmichele as they had been told to do. Around the third hour, they appeared before the Grain Council. "Go to our officer Messire Villano, and advise him as best you can about what we told you," said the Six. They all went before Messire Villano and said: "We are here before you; what do you want us to do or say?" Messire Villano replied: "Let us go inside, where we shall be more comfortable." So they all went up, and when they were inside the building where the Six met for their councils, Messire Villano had the doors locked, and had them come forward one by one; he called them and wrote down their names and then sent them into another room, which was sealed off. When he had written all their names and sent them all into the sealed room, he went off with two guards of the chief magistrate,

---

10. A man from the Umbrian town of Gubbio, from which many city-states in central Italy, especially Florence, hired strong, not particularly scrupulous officials.

Domenico Lenzi il Biadaiolo

for he was to dine with him at the palace. After a little while four policemen arrived and took two of the men away to the Stinche.[11] Little by little the palace guards began to arrive, and took three more men away to prison. Thus by twos and threes they were all taken to prison; in all 36 were arrested. The Grain Council ordered each of them to stand surety for five hundred pounds of grain, and they were carefully watched. This was an excellent thing.[12]

They stayed in prison until Wednesday night; at the first watch, several palace guards arrived and took four of the grain merchants to the place where the Grain Council met, where they were detained by Messire Villano; these four men were detained in separate places. Then Messire Villano called one of the four men, Dolce Guidicci, and began to torture him with a *colla*[13] without even questioning him first; and he tortured him mercilessly. Dolce cried out, "Sir, why do you torture me? What are you doing to me? What do you want of me? What have I done that you torture me so?" Messire Villano never ceased tugging on the rope; and the other three men, who were nearby, could hear the man screaming and crying, and were so afraid that they shook like leaves, even though they had committed no irregularities; for they knew that the same thing was going to happen to them.

When Dolce Guidicci had been tortured for quite a while and had screamed a good bit, Messire Villano had him lowered to the ground, and asked him: "Tell me how much grain or fodder each merchant has in his shop or house, who has bought grain in Florence in order to hoard it, and which grain merchants in Florence have been consorting with anyone who has been hoarding grain. All this I want to know. And you had better tell me, if you don't

---

11. The chief prison in Florence for debtors or people condemned to life imprisonment.

12. It might seem surprising that Lenzi, a *biadaiolo* (grain merchant) himself, should approve the arrest of 36 of his fellow merchants. But this is merely a particularly forceful example of the exaltation of the officials of the Florentine state (and hence of Florence herself) that is one of the main themes of Lenzi's book.

13. A rope run through a pulley, which when pulled lifted a suspect off the ground by his arms, which were tied behind his back.

want to stay hanging by your arms, and the torture to continue." Dolce answered fearfully and with humble words, saying: "May God help me if I don't tell you truthfully everything I know about what you've asked me." And he told the truth of what he knew, moaning and groaning all the while.

Then Messire Villano called the other three before him one by one and interrogated them in the same way. They told whatever they knew, and he kept them until Thursday at the first watch, when he sent them back to prison, and had four more men brought to him. These he tortured and interrogated as you have heard above, and sent them back to the prison in the same way.

The grain and fodder merchants sought the intercession of many of their friends; these were important men in Florence, who appeared before the Council and asked why they were being kept in prison. After much pleading, finally on Friday morning they were ordered to appear on Saturday, and each one was made to stand surety for five hundred pounds of grain or fodder that they could not buy in the city or countryside of Florence, nor sell or bargain for. So they were released under the condition that they would neither buy nor sell grain until Thursday, 15 October.

Paolo da Certaldo
Book of Good Practices

In the name of God amen.

1. In this book we shall give many good examples, practices, proverbs, and admonitions. Therefore, my son, brother, my good friend, neighbor, or comrade, or whoever you may be who read this book, listen well and understand what you shall find written here, and put it into action. Much good and honor will come to you, in body and soul.

89. So that your servants will be solicitous and useful to your household, always instruct them to not return home empty-handed. They should bring something with them when they return home, and especially when you are staying in the country. For it is well to bring all good things to a household.

152. When you buy grain, take care that they don't fill up the measure all at once, for two or three percent will always fall out. When you sell it, fill the measure all at once and you will get more grain out of it. But the middle course, the course of reason, is always the best; stick to that in all of your dealings, and you shall end well.

153. If you live off the income from your land and you aren't good at managing money (and one out of six men is not), don't sell your crops all at one time. For if you should invest the money in something else, and then not have money to live on, you might have to mortgage or sell off some of your land or chattels in order to live. In fact, you should calculate just how much money you need every month. If you are good at managing money, you still shouldn't sell all your crops at one time, to avoid going bankrupt. Sell them in four batches — in October, January, March, and May, always at the beginning of the month. Each time, sell a fourth, and you will get what you need out of your crops. Do the same for olive oil and wine and the other things produced on your land. Olive oil sells well during Lent, and in September; wine sells well from Lent until the end of August, if it is a wine that lasts. If it is a wine that should be drunk young, sell the must[1] separately, and the rest until the beginning of Lent.

246. When you buy land, be sure to have good, reliable guarantors, and make sure to obtain the necessary legal consent of women or children or other close relatives, so that you can't be cheated after the death of the seller.

251. If you are a merchant, and letters for you arrive along with other letters, always remember to read your own letters first before giving the other letters to the people to whom they are addressed. And if your letters should advise you to buy or sell some merchandise for your own advantage, call immediately for your agent, and do what the letters say, and then give the letters that came with yours. But don't give them until you have concluded your transactions, because those other letters might say things that could ruin your own dealings, and the service that you would have done to your friend or neighbor or some stranger would turn into great evil. You are not obliged to help others if it is a disservice to your own affairs.

---

1. The juice of grapes before it has fermented to produce wine.

270. If you have money that you want to invest in grain, buy small grains before you buy wheat, if you don't have much money; for you will make two *soldi* on every bushel of grain and only one on every bushel of wheat; and the grain will cost you a third of what the wheat would. Also, during times of shortage you'll find more buyers. And if you buy other goods, buy them when the prices are low and there is little demand for them, for in time you will derive profit from them, and you cannot lose in the process.

271. When you buy wine for your own use or for resale, always ask the man from whom you buy it how he treats the wine he keeps for himself and how much time it takes the wine to turn, and you do the same. Thus, you will not be deceived, and the wine won't go bad on you.

333. When you are in someone else's home, always take care not to speak ill of him. And take care not to say anything in the street or near a thin wall that you don't want everyone to know. Likewise, when you enter a room, don't speak or say anything until you know for certain who is in the room, for someone might be hiding behind the curtain or in some other concealed place, and could hear your business. As the saying goes, "Speak no lies when you're in the street." Never say anything in a place where you don't know that you cannot be heard by some man or woman whom you cannot see. If you wish to speak of secret things, speak softly, and in a place where the walls are so thick that you know that what you say will not be heard beyond the nearest wall. Or go to tell your secrets in a public square, or a meadow or beach or field, out in the open, so that you can see that there is no one nearby who can hear you. Beware of hedges and trees, and structures or walls or corners or any other place where someone can hide — man or woman, large or small — if you don't want your secrets to be known.

375. Be very careful when a man whom you do not know, nor whence he comes, is very kind to you and does you great honor and flatters and praises you both to your face and behind your

back; don't put your trust in him immediately. Don't say right away: "This is the best friend I've got." First you must test him, not once but a hundred times — that is to say, many times. You must test him in many ways and in many situations before you accept him as a true friend. And I tell you that you should always hold back a little; even if you trust this man, don't trust him totally, for there are many examples of men who have trusted totally and have been deceived, especially where money is involved. I'll give you this example: there is no horse so loyal nor so good in the bridle, which when ridden for a long time without reining it in will not become spoiled. The same occurs with men: the son is subject to and obedient and humble with his father as long as his father has control of the household and his possessions; but when the father has given his son the authority to control his own possessions, he outstrips his father and hates him and can't wait for him to die so that he won't have to bear the sight of him any more. And while he was a friend before, he becomes your enemy because of the trust you have placed in him. So, since I forbid you to trust totally in your own children, you must be even more wary of people whom you don't know. "He who trusts not, will not be deceived," says the proverb. Now, I am not saying that you should be completely distrustful, but rather that there should be a happy medium in all things. If you always keep to this happy medium in every aspect of your life, you shall be praised and considered wise. Refrain from both immoderation and excessive moderation; but if you have to sin in one, exceed in moderation rather than in immoderation.

388. I said earlier in this book that the soul should have two spiritual eyes, one kept open to Heaven, hoping for eternal life, and the other open to the fear of the sufferings of Hell. If you do this, you will never do an evil thing, out of fear of the torments of Hell. But what good will it do you to not do evil things out of fear of the sufferings of Hell and to merely hope passively for the glory of eternal life? Surely, if you ever hope to go to Heaven, it will do you no good not to do evil, if you don't do good deeds as well. Our souls should fear Hell and its torments; and, as I have

said, always have an eye on those torments, and they shall never sin out of that fear. But the other eye should be kept on God, and not only out of hope, which would deceive our souls, but out of love and charity. We must serve God with good actions and good thoughts. With good works, the soul acquires merit; and by acquiring merit in this life, in the next life the soul shall bask in the glory for which it had hoped. With hope alone, and no good works, our souls would not attain that glory, and would be disappointed in the end.

Giovanni di Pagolo Morelli
Ricordi

The Beauty and Goodness of the Land, People, and Fortifications of the Mugello

I shall begin by saying that the Mugello is the most beautiful place in the Tuscan countryside, and it is reputed thus by the greater part of the citizens of Florence. Although this testimonial is quite adequate, nevertheless for the greater glory of the Mugello I do not wish to limit myself to saying this, but shall go into greater detail at various points in these pages. To my mind, in order to fully demonstrate what I have said, one should speak of the main points, which encompass everything. First, we must see and examine the people who own property and govern the place; second, what is owned, which we shall divide into two parts — that is, first we shall tell about the lands and then about the buildings, because each has different parts. Now I have established how we shall proceed in the following sections.

The beauty of the Mugello can be seen clearly and manifestly in its people, for there are a great number of men who are farmers and honorable men, proper and upright in their profession; likewise their womenfolk are comely countrywomen, cheerful and pleasant, all very affectionate, always singing and dancing and rejoicing. Likewise there are many noble citizens, men and women of all ages, who make the countryside blossom with their hunting and birding and banqueting and courtly life all the year round.

Then look at the countryside itself, which is so charming and pleasant, with all the pleasures you could think to ask for. The Mugello is situated in the middle of a beautiful cultivated plain adorned with delightful fruit trees, all cared for and as beautiful as a garden. An enchanting little river[1] runs through it, and along its banks are nurseries that slope down from the lovely hills that surround the plain. All around, like a pretty garland, are slopes and hills for climbing; there are also high mountains that are no less enchanting.[2] There are wild parts and cultivated parts of the Mugello, and some are neither wild nor cultivated, but all are very lovely. The lands near the dwelling places are well kept, adorned with fruit trees and beautiful vineyards, and numerous fresh-water pools or springs. The hills are wilder, with woods and forests with many chestnut trees that provide a great abundance of fine fat chestnuts and maroons. There is a great deal of game in these woods, such as wild boar, deer, bears, and other wild beasts. Near the dwelling places there are many lovely oak groves; some of the people who live there have arranged these groves as places of pleasure, clearing the ground so that one can walk barefoot beneath the trees with no fear of hurting one's feet. You also see big groves of broom trees, where there are large numbers of hares, pheasants, and other game. Closer to the dwelling places, you see large fields of fragrant herbs — thyme, veronica, strawflowers, and juniper, with charming springs that flow everywhere. The area is full of partridges, quail, pheasant, and hares. It is a delightful place to hunt.

Third and last are the buildings, which are large, strong, and well situated, with noble walls. There are many spacious homes,

---

1. The Sieve.
2. This joyous, not particularly realistic depiction of the Mugello as a *locus amoenus* is one of the strongest echoes of Boccaccio in Morelli's prose (see the conclusion to Day VI of the *Decameron*).

surrounded by rich, charming places in which to walk and amuse oneself.

 To give this last part, which is no less lovely than the others, its due, I shall describe it in some detail. In the center of the built area, where the leader lives, there are six main fortresses, placed by the government of Florence to guard and protect the whole area. These castles are built on lovely sites, nobly arranged in the center of the plain, about three miles apart. They are surrounded by wide, dark moats full of good water, and are bounded by high, thick, strong walls surmounted by sturdy towers with high corbels. Inside the castle walls are numerous houses arranged in charming neighborhoods abounding in decorations of every kind. The people who live there are wise and experienced and know how to receive strangers honorably. In an area of about two or three miles surrounding these castles, on the plains and hills and slopes, there are many dwellings of citizens in charming, delightful locations, with lovely views of the fields and gardens and meadows. The houses are large, with halls and chambers worthy of great lords, and pools of clear, cool water. On the higher slopes, six or eight miles from the castles, are many large, noble fortresses owned by noble gentlemen, who attract the peasants by giving them official appointments, honoring them so that they are glad to stay in these fortresses with them for company and for pleasure. In the wilder places and where it is necessary, there are many fortresses kept and guarded by our government, which are marvelously strong and fine and suited to the needs of the peasants. One couldn't write fully about all the beauties of this place on six sheets; so I shall bring this description to a close, and settle for having only touched upon some of them.

The goodness of the Mugello is shown chiefly in its people; this is manifestly clear. Firstly, they are devout, charitable people, according to their station in life. This can be seen in the many places of devotion that have been built, and the great aid and alms given by the people to support these places. Among others, there are the hermits of Monte Asinaio,[3] who are very devout; there are also the Franciscan friars at Bosco ai Frati, near San Piero a Sieve, a place of great devotion. And there are many others.

You will also find many people who are faithful to the Florentine state and to the Guelph party; they have shown their faithfulness on many occasions and in their good deeds. Among other things, with the help of Florence and their own vigilance, they drove out the tyrannical Ubaldini,[4] who are Ghibellines, enemies of the Guelphs and of the Florentine State. Our allies in the Mugello received great damage to their people and property at the hands of the Ubaldini, and were involved in many skirmishes with them. These country dwellers were strong and faithful in their devotion to Florence, and never capitulated to the many promises and large gifts with which the Ubaldini attempted to bribe them. They have always been against the Ubaldini, and it is never necessary to alert them to defend the lands and castles, for they have always lovingly and zealously followed the triumphal banner of our city-state and likewise the Catholic banner of the venerable Guelph party. They are likewise faithful to each citizen of Florence individually; they are loyal and upright in their professions; diligent in their work; well-mannered, pleasant, reverent, and full of courtesy; knowledgeable about all things, but especially those that delight gentle folk, such as hunting for game and birds, and fishing. They are always ready with the appropriate persons and things for whatever you request. Their womenfolk, like the men, are well-mannered, pleasant, honest, wise, and hard-working, with all the virtues desirable in country folk.

The great bounty of their abundant harvests can be seen in their lands. On the plain of the Mugello, you see the best and most bounteous fruit-bearing lands in the Florentine countryside, where

---

3. Mount Senario, to the North of Florence, famous in Italian literature for the story of the young man and the "geese" (*Decameron* day IV, introduction); it was the site of a colony of hermits, and later of a famous monastery.

4. The Ubaldini were a powerful family that dominated the Tuscan-Emilian Apennines; often allied with the Romagnoles and Ghibellines against Florence, they were repeatedly defeated by the Florentines from 1251 onward, and their castles were dismantled between 1358 and 1373.

you will see two or three generous crops harvested each year. Anything you could wish for is raised there to perfection. The lands on the slopes are perfect; a great abundance of wheat and grain and fruit and olives is grown there, as well as a great quantity of wine grapes, wood, and chestnuts, and enough livestock to supply a third of Florence's demand. The Mugello also produces a great quantity of cheese and a great deal of lambswool cloth, chickens and other domesticated fowl, as well as game in great abundance. And all of these things are supremely good, better than anything else in the Florentine countryside.

Cardinal Ottaviano degli Ubaldini

At the time when the Ubaldini family were lords of the Mugello — or rather, of the Tuscan Apennine — one of them was made a cardinal, and was called Cardinal Ottaviano.[5] He was a haughty, almost tyrannical man, enjoyed great wealth, and was not at all a model of ecclesiastical restraint. While he was with the Pope, who then had his curia at Avignon,[6] Cardinal Ottaviano got the idea, in his tyrannical aspirations, to build a fabulous fortress in the Mugello or rather in the Apennine. He quickly began to carry out his idea, first consulting with the great master builders and with wise, experienced military men. With their advice, he had a castle designed with all of the noble appurtenances and fortifications that could be devised. Having determined what was the strongest and best situated place in the Mugello for such a fortress, he sent his ambassador and the master builders with the designs to his relations, instructing them to build the fortress on

---

5. The famous Ottaviano or Attaviano degli Ubaldini, who was bishop of Bologna from 1240 to 1244, cardinal from 1245 on, and died in 1273. In Dante's *Inferno*, Farinata degli Uberti shows Ottaviano to Dante among the heretics, along with Frederick II.

6. The Pope actually was not residing at Avignon at this time.

Montaccianico, according to the designs. They were all exceedingly pleased with the idea, and began immediately to build it. So with all the greatest master builders of Tuscany and with the help of everybody on the mountain, where there was a large number of people, the fortress was built and completed and furnished with every appurtenance for its defense. In addition to the fortress, the mountain itself was so well fortified that with no danger of any impediment, sufficient provisions of wheat, grain, wine, and other things were gathered every year on Montaccianico to amply provide for the men who were needed to guard it.

Finally, when Cardinal Ottaviano heard that his fortress was built and that it was surpassingly fine and strong, he had the audacity to invite the Pope[7] and all his court to see it, with these very words: "Holy Father, I have had a fortress built that is one of the most marvelous in the world. It has a lush, elegant garden, twenty-five miles long and eighteen miles wide, all enclosed by high, strong walls. May it please Your Holiness to come and see it." With these and other fawning words, he made the Pope and his brother cardinals and all the papal court long to see this place. Once they had promised to come, he ordered that on the plain of the Mugello, where there is a church called the Holy Cross, there be built several large, beautiful, spacious palaces; he did this so that the Pope and his court would have a fitting place to stay. When it was all ready, the Pope and all the cardinals and many other high-ranking prelates came from Avignon to see the castle and its garden, which took up almost the whole Mugello. Its walls were the surrounding hills, which are situated just as if they were real walls. When they had seen the castle and the garden, they all agreed that it was just as Cardinal Ubaldini had described it, and the court remained at Holy Cross for several days, with great pleasure, and then went on to Rome.

When Cardinal Ubaldini died (I don't know how long he lived after this, or if the Pope was the same), the Pope consulted with

---

7. Pope Gregory X, who passed through Florence and the Mugello in 1273 on his way from Rome to Lyon. Giovanni Villani (VII, 42) also has a long section on this episode.

Giovanni di Pagolo Morelli

his cardinals, and it was decreed that there could never be another cardinal from the Ubaldini family, on account of the man's capricious, exceedingly proud ways. And it has ever been so, by the grace of God.

The magnificent, sublime people and state of Florence have always been enemies and persecutors and destroyers of iniquitous tyrants, robbers, and destroyers of the people, and especially enemies of the Ghibellines.[8] When they saw and heard of the tyranny, theft, and outrages that the Ubaldini, tyrants of the Tuscan Apennine and of the Mugello, were committing, they determined to extinguish that thievery as they had extinguished many others in the area (they had already taken many of the Ubaldini's castles, but the Ubaldini still had many others, especially the one on Montaccianico, of which they were exceedingly proud). The Florentines decided to take the fortress on Montaccianico from the Ubaldini, and in the year of Our Lord 1300 or thereabouts, they laid seige to it.[9] The castle called La Scarperia acted almost as a stockade for the Florentines as they waged war against the Castle of Montaccianico. The seige lasted seventeen years before the Florentines took the fortress, and then a treaty was made. In truth, force of arms was of little avail, for it was like waging war against one of the stars in the sky. But it pleased Our Lord God, help and defender of all good, that the Florentines should capture

---

8. The Guelphs and the Ghibellines were rival political factions in northern and central Italy from about the twelfth to the fifteenth century. These parties originated in Germany in the early twelfth century during a struggle for the throne of the Holy Roman Empire between two noble houses. In the thirteenth century, the Guelphs were the party that opposed the authority of the Holy Roman emperors in Italy and supported the papacy, while the Ghibellines supported the imperial authority. In the fourteenth century, after the emperors had ceased to be a major power in Italy, the contest degenerated into a struggle of local political factions, as described here by Morelli. In 1334 Pope Benedict XII forbade the further use of the Guelph and Ghibelline names, but they were occasionally used as late as the sixteenth century.

9. The seige of the fortress of Montaccianico took place in 1306, and lasted from April through September (not the seventeen years of Morelli's extravagant retelling). Villani (VIII, 86) gives a detailed account of it.

that fortress and many others with great honor and victory. Some of the fortresses were dismantled, as they were costly to guard and were thought to be superfluous and of no usefulness to the State.

Later, on account of the wars we had with the Visconti of Milan (some of which you shall hear about here below), it was deemed best to dismantle all of the fortresses because of the expense of guarding them and the great dangers that would arise should one of them be lost to our enemies. So all of the fortresses in which the Ubaldini had lived in the Tuscan Apennine were dismantled, also in part so that the Ubaldini wouldn't think about trying to regain them for the income they could provide. But then it happened that in the third war that Florence had with the Duke of Milan, we lost Bologna to him, and with the Duke's help some of the descendents of the Ubaldini came to the Apennine and almost won back their former land in the mountains and villages; and certain stockades that they had were a worry to Florence. This had come about because there were no fortresses left from which to put up a resistance; so the Florentines realized that it had been a mistake to dismantle them all. It is impossible to foretell future events without great foresight; one would practically have to be a soothsayer. Thus it is important to take counsel with old men, who are wise and experienced and have seen many things. One must not be precipitate the moment one gets an idea, but should ponder it for a long while and follow reason and counsel rather than one's own wishes or desires.

Pagolo di Bartolomeo Morelli

Bartolomeo's fourth and last son was named Pagolo Morelli. Although he was the youngest, it seems fitting to me for no other reason than for his virtues, to honor him by remembering some of his openhearted, serviceable, wise, good acts, which were so many and such that my mind is incapable of comprehending them. But failing to record his great, lofty deeds would not be

Giovanni di Pagolo Morelli

honoring them, but rather diminishing his honor, even though I could never write about him on the level he deserves.

Pagolo Morelli was born in the year of Our Lord 1335, or thereabouts; I believe that some daughters were born to Bartolomeo between Dino and Pagolo. According to what I heard our mother say, Pagolo never saw Bartolomeo, his father; it seems this happened because Pagolo was sent out to a wet nurse in the Mugello and kept there until he was quite grown. Pagolo told our mother that this nurse of his was the strangest, most beastly woman that ever lived, and that she had beaten him so much that just remembering it made him so angry that if she had been within his reach at that moment he would have killed her. These memories of his, and the fact that he said "I never saw my father," tell me that he lived for a long time in the country. And I believe that since Bartolomeo already had older sons who were on their way to becoming men, as you have heard before, he didn't trouble himself much about this youngest one. Perhaps since the boy's mother was already dead, and Bartolomeo was an old man by then, he didn't want the trouble of raising him; and to save money, or for whatever reason, it happened the way I've said. As I understand it, when Pagolo returned from the Mugello, his father was already dead; Pagolo must have been ten or twelve years old by that time. Just think, having always, or most of the time, lived in the country, what he must have been like — little better than a peasant! But Nature, which is gentle in itself, always attracts virtue, and those who develop late because of neglect soon recover their breeding. The reasons for this are clear, and shown by effects. That is just what happened to this boy, who had been abandoned, and with the help of God I will tell about some of these things so that his descendants may remember them.

The boy returned to Florence; he was as pure and simple as he was courteous and intelligent. He found himself fatherless, in the hands of his older brothers, who had taken their father's entire estate for their own, and didn't bother much about their younger brother, whom they left on his own, doing little to help him along. But as simple and unpolished as he was, on account of having had such a poor upbringing in the country, Pagolo decided by himself to go to school and learn to read and write. Because he was so inexperienced, and was ashamed of being older than the other students, the schoolmaster beat him; so he left the school and did not return. For this reason, Pagolo changed schools on his own many times. According to his wife, Madonna Telda, with some schools he made an agreement that they shouldn't beat him. If they kept the agreement, he would stay; if not, he left. In this way he learned to read and write and do sums; he had a very good memory, and was driven solely by his own virtuous will, desirous to learn and to make up for lost time. When with the help of God he had reached the age of eighteen years or more, he desired his brothers to give him his own share of the business; before that, he had worked with them on salary for a few years in their warehouse. Since his three older brothers had already taken over almost the whole of their father's estate for themselves, there was no one to look out for Pagolo except himself, and reason. And although he tried to stand up for himself, they paid him little heed, and he got nothing from them, either because he didn't understand his rights or because he was still inexperienced and timorous. In the end, they assigned what they pleased to him from his father's estate: some land in the Mugello, a portion of some houses they had in Florence, and about five hundred florins in cash. He remained a partner of Giovanni and Dino at the warehouse. Pagolo stayed there with them for several years on a salary, as we find in his books. He was never able to get any of the money assigned to him without a struggle, and with no benefit or profit to himself. His salary was all promised to him, but only a part of it was actually paid. He later went into business on his own, except for a certain period of time when he and Dino went back into business together, each putting in half of the money. Giovanni was the one who made the most money; Pagolo made out the worst of all.

But he tried to better himself as much as he could. When he reached his majority, he complained to his relatives and friends and made several deals with Giovanni and the others, and managed to accomplish many things. Be he always got the short end of the stick, because Giovanni was a grown man, cunning and experienced in the ways of the world, as were the other brothers.

Giovanni di Pagolo Morelli

Giovanni was the eldest; the business was in his hands, and he could make people believe what he wished — they gave him more credence. Because he was the eldest, he had a wife; the relatives helped him, and he had many advantages. Pagolo, who by his own talents showed himself to be diligent about his business, wasn't listened to or supported except in part, and more out of conscience than out of willingness or love, for he wasn't held in as high esteem as Giovanni and the other brothers.

Fortune and his own industry and hard work favored him; for he never wasted a moment of time, and was always careful to win the love of God his Creator by his almsgiving and good works, and by winning the friendship of good men as well as respectable and powerful ones. He frequented such men, showing his great friendship by being of service to them in anything he could, asking their advice about his affairs, and showing his faith and hope in them. He honored them by inviting them to dine, and in many other ways. He acted as godfather to their children and similar and even greater things, as occur every day when one frequents people with whom one wishes to ingratiate onself. In this manner, and in other prudent, far-seeing ways, he was able to win such friends that at the time of his greatest need, as I shall tell, they — and not his relations — helped and supported him so that ultimately he was not wronged, chiefly through the aid and will of God, without whom nothing can be accomplished. If we wished to be faithful Christians and friends of God, we would acknowledge His power and supreme justice every day; but we are blinded by our sins and would rather judge and believe that good or bad fortune befalls us either by chance or on account of our greater or lesser intelligence, rather than by the will of God. But this is not true, for everything proceeds from God, according to our just deserts. Therefore I say that wise men have an advantage, for they know God and act well and help themselves better. For God helps those who help themselves, and who accomplish things through their own toil. This can be seen clearly and manifestly in Pagolo, as you shall hear.

You have already heard about the behavior of Pagolo's elder brothers toward him, and how all three of them died and how they had arranged their affairs. Along with several others, Pagolo was named conservator of his brothers' heirs, and inherited half of two of the brothers' estates, as I have already recounted. Pagolo, who was still really a boy, had to take care of everything. With God's help, I hope to tell you how difficult and risky it was, so that you will be able to picture it all. Pagolo's brothers died at the height of the epidemic of 1363; after contracting the plague, they went to God in the space of twenty days. As you have already heard, two of them were involved in the dye trade, in which they had invested around fifteen thousand florins. The third brother, Giovanni, who was the first to die, had a young wife, who survived him. Giovanni was involved in usury, and little else; and not only in Florence, but throughout the whole surrounding countryside, mostly with laborers and poor people, as well as with great, powerful men both inside and outside of Florence. At the time of the plague, Pagolo — young, inexperienced, and alone, with only the help and advice of his friends, shaken by the death of his relations and fearful for his own life, found himself embroiled in thousands of florins of debits and credits; many of his brothers' creditors and agents had died, and he had to search not only in Florence and the surrounding countryside, but also in Arezzo, Borgo San Lorenzo, Siena, Pisa, and other places, in order to locate merchandise, sell it, and keep everything going, which he did with great diligence and much toil. Just think how you would feel if you found yourself in such times and with such a job to carry out! And yet Pagolo took care of everything, from the biggest task to the smallest, well and assiduously. All at the same time, he had to repay five hundred florins to Calandro's wife; to inventory his brothers' belongings and homes; and to take care of the funeral arrangements, bequests, and all the other things that have to be done at such times. He had to contend with female relatives, with grown children about the disposition of their fathers' estates, with conservators and with other relatives. And, as you shall hear, all the relatives were standing by ready to steal whatever they could and to annoy Pagolo and interrupt what he was trying to accomplish. He had to cash out their capital, and the money that Calandro had lent in places all over Florence and the countryside. He had to negotiate with the bishop and with the most powerful men in Florence; he called in all debts, no matter who owed them. He carefully undeceived everyone at the bishop's court, including the bishop himself. At the papal court, he achieved his goal, even though he had many people against him. And he did all this not through the power of money, but through his own reason and diligence. Besides this, he dealt in the wool trade with Tommaso di Guccio and others. He dabbled in the Public Fund and negotiated several thousand florins in personal loans and letters of credit; he traded in French fabrics and many other things. Around this time he took to wife the daughter of Matteo di More Quaratesi,[10] Madonna Telda, a beautiful girl thirteen years of age or younger. You will find the date and the amount of the dowry written in his papers. He pledged his troth to her on the 13th of December 1663, the feastday of St. Lucy, and married her on January 17, 1364. The marriage certificate was drafted by Messire Francesco di Messire Gianni d'Antica. Pagolo paid the marriage tax on the 21st of February, 1634, as indicated in his Book A, folio 109.

Just when he had taken care of all his brothers' affairs, through no one's toil but his own, and thought he might rest a little, Giovanni's widow, with her brother, Niccolò Bagnesi, acting in collusion with the other conservators, went after Pagolo in an attempt to wrest from him the money and the guardianship of Giovanni's children; they made many false allegations against Pagolo, as he carefully noted in his papers. He himself recorded the final decision of the court about all of this. To further their cause, unbeknowst to Pagolo and with the advice of Madonna Lisa and the others, they married Giovanni's son Bernardo to the daughter of Gucciozzo de' Ricci in order to have more support against Pagolo; for Gucciozzo was a powerful citizen, feared by many and possessed of every worldly good.[11] With all their own

---

10. A prominent family in the Black Guelph faction, already wealthy by the early 1300s (Compagni, III, 7).

11. The Ricci were a powerful family belonging to the White Guelph faction (Villani, VIII, 71); Gucciozzo was the head of a rich, prosperous company.

power and that of their relatives and friends, they took Pagolo to law several times, using every dishonest trick they could. In the end, they were shamed, with the help of God and of the right, as well as Pagolo's friends and his own constancy and virtue, as he especially recorded in his own papers. Thus it is unnecessary for me to go into any further detail about this.

Around this time, Pagolo's family began to grow; he and his wife had five children, first two girls and then three boys, about whom I shall write at the proper time. Pagolo conducted himself well and wisely in all of his affairs, applying himself to noble, virtuous things. If it had pleased God to give him even ten more years of life, he would have become rich to the tune of more than fifty thousand florins, and would have had a large family, for he had at least one child every year. He would have taken part in affairs of state for every good reason and cause. His name had already been put in for the election of 1366 by Dino di Geri Cigliamochi, who was one of the Priors at that time (he was Pagolo's uncle). His name was chosen as one of the Priors after his death; I think he was the first of our ancestors to be named a Prior.

It pleased Our Lord that Pagolo should render his soul up to God just when he was about to flourish in all of his affairs, on the 14th of June, 1374. He had been married about ten and a half years earlier, for he had married his wife on January 18, 1363. He left an estate of twenty thousand florins. His soul was well and devoutly disposed, as can be seen in his last will and testament. Pagolo was a man of good character, very loving and charitable. He never refused anything that was asked of him, neither from a poor man nor a rich one, and was especially generous with money. He was a good relative to those who didn't attempt to undermine him. He died of the plague, and his body was interred with great honor in the church of Santa Croce, beside those of his father and brothers. He was survived by two daughters and two sons, three of whom were still nursing. I shall write about them in the proper place and time.

Giovanni di Pagolo Morelli

Bartolomea di Pagolo Morelli

The first fruit of Pagolo's marriage was a baby girl; she was born on Monday, June 23rd, at seven thirty, in the year of Our Lord 1365. She was baptized in the baptistery of San Giovanni the following Saturday morning, the 28th of that month. The names given to her were Giovanna and Bartolomea; Lione Lioni, Tommaso di Bese Busini, and the innkeeper Francesco Brunellini acted as her godfathers. She was always called Mea.

Mea was of ordinary height, with beautiful blond hair, a very fine figure, and so amiable that she dripped with charm. Her hands were like ivory, and so shapely that they seemd to have been painted by Giotto; they were long and soft, with tapering fingers and long, shapely nails, pink and clear. Her beauty was matched by her talents, for she could do any kind of women's work with her own hands; she was extremely adept in everything she did. Her speech was refined and pleasing, her actions pure and temperate, her words effectual. She was a spirited, frank women with the mettle of a man, and abounded in every virtue. She could read and write as well as any man; she sang and danced perfectly, and could have served men or women at table as adroitly as any young man used to serving at wedding banquets or similar occasions. She was expert at running a household, without a hint of avariciousness or stinginess. But she made the most of everything, admonishing and guiding her household with good teachings and her own good example, living a joyful, happy life. She wisely set about making all of the various members of her household happy, allaying every trouble, anger, or sadness that she might see in any of them. She handled everything wisely and with benevolence, and, as you shall see, she had to deal with her husband's family, which was large and unruly.

The conservators of his family and hers arranged for Mea to be married to Antonio d'Agnolo Barucci; she had a dowry of one thousand five hundred florins. Antonio lived with his father and mother, who were quite old, but prosperous, and with a wretched brother of his, who also took a wife at the same time. They also had two sisters, both grown and married, and two nephews, good youths, by one of the sisters. I have told all this so that I might return to what I said before: that Mea, wise and discerning as she was, was loved by everyone, although there was little harmony among the other members of the family. Her goodness was the more commendable, for where there was great discord and scandal, she alone was loved by all. She managed to bring peace and harmony to many unpleasant situations among them.

Mea was married in 1380, and Antonio and his brother Francesco made a great, joyful celebration. At that time the Barucci family lived in great state and had a fortune of twenty thousand florins; they were wool merchants, much loved by everyone, wise, pleasant, and very respectable. Mea had four children with Antonio, but none of them lived longer than two years; the last, a baby boy, was born on the 8th of February, 1387, and was named Agnolo. Mea had been unwell for about a week when she gave birth to this baby in the eighth month of her pregnancy; she never recovered, but died of that same illness on Saturday the 15th of February, at the eighth hour. The baby died the next day, so Mea left no offspring. She was buried in the church of Santa Croce, under the transept, on the left side of Agnolo Barucci's tomb.

As you enter under the transept of the church, there is a door that leads to a sort of vault on the right side, along the wall. I want to describe this very clearly, for seeing where her bones are buried should make us all think of her goodness. I especially entreat everyone who is descended from Pagolo Morelli to go and see the place where Mea lies, at least on All Souls Day, and to pray to God for the well-being of her soul. For the true light and fruit of her soul are prayer and almsgiving; may God grant that they help her blessed soul.

Giovanni di Pagolo Morelli

It pleased our Lord God to grant to Pagolo Morelli our father a fourth child, a son, with his wife Madonna Telda. He was born on Thursday evening, the thirtieth of October, in the year of Our Lord 1371, at 1/3 past the twenty-fourth hour. He was baptized the following Saturday, the first of November, that is, the day of the feast of All Saints. His godfathers were Giovanni d'Andrea, Lorenzo di Tennia, and the dyer Raffaello, all from the neighborhood of San Jacopo, bosom friends of Pagolo Morelli. He was given the names Giovanni and Simone: Giovanni for his uncle, Pagolo's brother, and Simone because he was born on the feast day of St. Simon.

Giovanni di Pagolo was of average height and complexion; he had beautiful hair and was a little rubicund in the face. He was not strong by nature, not a big eater, and of gentle blood. He was displeased by evil things, especially those that brought harm or shame to his City. He denounced such things whenever he had occasion to discourse about them; likewise, he would take steps to correct them if it were in his power to do so.[12] He wished to live an honorable life, never going against whoever was in power in word or deed. He frequented the good old men of Florence, Guelphs loyal to the city-state. He never thought or desired anything but honor, state, and greatness for Florence. Of the new breed of Florentines, artisans and small-scale traders, he demanded duty, peace, and harmony. He did not like everything about their behavior, but he did mingle with them in some things; for it is good to keep in touch with the humbler folk. He always devotedly embraced the holy Catholic Guelph party — may God keep it as His devoted standard-bearer, for it has always defended the Holy Church. Up to this day it has not yet pleased God that Giovanni be able to show his good will toward Florence and

---

12. In writing about himself, Giovanni di Pagolo adopted a deliberately impersonal tone; but his moral and political attitudes come through clearly.

toward her good citizens and merchants in a concrete way, but presumably He has done this for the best.[13]

Advice to the Novice Merchant

If you decide to deal in wool or French fabrics, do everything yourself, and don't expect to get rich in two days. Use your own money; don't ever borrow money to make money. Deal with people you can trust and who have a good reputation and credit, and whose affairs are out in the open. And if on some occasion you find that you have been swindled by someone, don't ever fall into his hands again. Don't believe it when someone offers you too much for your merchandise; don't be deceived by inflated prices. Always demand everything clearly in writing. Do less at first; play it safe.

If you go into the wool trade, do so with your own money; don't be eager to send out your merchandise if you don't have someone who is as interested in your affairs as you yourself are. If you can do without partners, do so; if not, choose your partner well — a good man, and with plenty of money. Don't choose someone above your station or from an uppity family. Don't go into any business or trade that you don't understand; do something that you know how to do, and stay away from things that you don't, for you will surely be duped. If you want to learn about anything, do so from the bottom up: frequent men in warehouses and counting houses, and go out and familiarize yourself with merchants and merchandise; see with your own eyes the places where you intend to do business.

Test your friends, or those who you consider to be your friends, a hundred times, before you trust them. Never trust anyone to the point that he could unmake you. Be wary about trusting people;

---

13. Up to this time, Giovanni had not held any public office; the first office he held was Company Standard-bearer, in 1409.

don't be gullible. Whoever shows most by his words that he is loyal and wise, trust him the least. And trust in no way anyone who proffers himself to you. Enjoy listening to big talkers, braggarts, and showoffs, and give as good as you get, but don't believe anything they say that might bring harm to you, and don't trust them at all. Don't trust sanctimonious men, sycophants, or hypocrites who cover themselves with a priest's mantle; you're better off trusting a soldier. Don't have anything to do with a man who has changed businesses or partners or masters many times, nor with a man who gambles, goes whoring (especially with males), dresses too extravagantly, dines too well, or is flighty; don't get involved with such men by entrusting your money or merchandise to them, or putting your affairs in their hands.

If you trade outside of Florence, go in person often, at least once a year, to those places, to see what is going on and to settle your accounts. Observe how those who represent you live, and if they are spendthrifts; make sure they keep good credit, that they don't fling themselves into deals nor get in too deep. Make sure they are solid businessmen and don't go beyond their mandate. The moment they cross you in anything, get rid of them. Always conduct yourself wisely, don't get too involved, nor ever show off your wealth; keep it secret and always try to give the impression that you have half as much as you really do. If you maintain this style of life you will never be duped too much, nor will those who come after you. Be sure that what you do is written out extensively in your books; never spare your pen. In this way you shall make money without too much risk; you shall avoid disputes and swindles, and you won't need to fear having to make restitution or that your children should be asked to do so. You shall live free, since you shall be firm and solid in your holdings, and with no worries.

In addition to this, you must take care not to leave your children with too many obligations. Since they will of necessity have to take from your estate to handle the necessary things when you die, you don't want to add too many things to what they have to pay, which is much more difficult to do than to say. Give alms when you are healthy; they will be more pleasing to God and will do less harm to your children. And if you do leave obligations, give them a specific time span; never, never leave any obligation in perpetuity; designate an end to what you want to be done. In leaving your estate, don't base yourself on your entire capital, especially if your children are quite young; reduce it by one fourth of your net worth. If you base yourself on this, you won't go wrong.

Designate only a few people, good ones, as guardians of your children. If you are a merchant and your trustees don't know anything about the trade, let them take your share out of the business. If you leave cash and your children have quite a bit of property, let them take what they need and put the rest in good, well-documented investments, as long as all the trustees are in agreement. Make it clear in your will that none of the trustees or their relatives can have what you leave to your children, and if they do they must be held totally responsible. But if the trustees come to realize that their wards are ill-equipped to manage their own money, and more likely to spend, gamble, and eat up their inheritance than to keep it, in this case for the good of the wards, the trustees should spend the money to buy property near Florence, good land not too close to the river, in places where there are plenty of laborers; they should buy property that they can turn around and re-sell at any time. If you take this course, I truly believe that it will be the best for your young heirs.

※

After you have completed your schooling, endeavor to study Virgil, Boethius, Seneca or other authors for at least an hour every day, as if you were still in school. This will result in great benefit to your mind: by studying the teachings of these authors, you shall know how you should act in your present life, both for the health of your soul and for the usefulness and honor of your body. And although when you are young this might seem rather difficult and burdensome, when you come of age and your intellect begins to savor the reason for things and the sweetness of knowledge, you shall derive as much pleasure out of it, as much delight, as much consolation as you do out of anything in the world. You shall not prize so much wealth, children, status or any great or honorable preeminence, once you have knowledge and can repute yourself a man and not a beast. Knowledge is what shall bring you to a high, honored place; virtue and your own intellect shall lead you there, whether or not you wish it. You shall have all the great men at your disposal: you can be with Virgil in your study as long as you want; he won't tell you no, but will answer your questions and will advise and teach you at no cost whatsoever; he shall take away your melancholy thoughts, and give you pleasure and consolation. You can be with Boethius, with Dante and the other poets, with Tulio, who will teach you perfect diction; with Aristotle, who will teach you philosophy. You shall know the reason for things, and every little thing shall give you the greatest pleasure. You shall be with the blessed prophets in the Holy Scripture, you shall read and study the Bible, you shall learn of the great acts of those holy prophets, you shall be fully instructed in the faith and the advent of the Son of God, your soul shall have great consolation, you shall not suffer no matter what befalls you. You shall be open-hearted and know which remedies are good and healthy. You shall be so well instructed and knowledgeable that it would be superfluous to say more.

But because we are prone to vice and full of deceit and betrayal, I shall inform you of certain actions and precautions with which you shall humble the evil, leading them back in part to your own benevolence or redressing their evil actions, in this way: in your relationships, lean chiefly on those who are in power and belong to the Guelph party and have good credibility and no stains on their reputation. If you can't get to such people through your relatives, become their friend by speaking well of them, serving them wherever it is in your power, seeking them out, and offering to do things for them. Frequent such men, but try to get closer to one or two of them who you can see have power. Once you have made sure that they are not corrupt, seek their advice; show them your faith in and affection for them; invite them to dine at your home and do things for them that you believe will please them and make them condescend to be your friend, even if it costs you a little. In addition, try to stay close to whoever is in power in the Public Palace and the Signory, and obey and follow their wishes and commands. Be careful not to speak ill of their undertakings, even if they are not good; hold your tongue, and don't speak except to commend them. Refuse to hear or do anything against them in any way, even if you should be insulted by them. If anyone should mention to you anything against whoever is in power, refuse to listen, and avoid them at all costs. Don't consort or have relationships with malcontents, and don't hold discourse with them except in the presence of others who participate in the government of the State. But if by some misfortune you should hear something ill of them, report it immediately and without a second thought to the Signory or to the office charged with protecting the city. Thus should you endeavor to live upright and in the clear so that nothing shall stain your reputation in any way, and especially anything that might be against the Guelph party.

You should also endeavor to ingratiate yourself with all types of people, and this is the way: offend no one in word or deed, neither by shaming them or impugning their honor or harming their property or person. Because there are deceitful people in Florence who will try every trick to corrupt you, and because you can't recognize all of them, always speak well of everyone and don't agree with those who speak ill of others; either hold your tongue, or speak well. Be pleasing in your discourse; say things that will gratify the company you are with; be courteous to every kind of person; be hospitable to them, give them to eat and drink; by day and night consort with your neighbors in Florence and in the countryside; serve them however you can. If you realize that someone in your circle is bad, pretend not to know, but be wary of him and don't trust him a jot. Be brave and courageous in defending your honor and your rights; demand them openly, reasonably and with confidence, with legitimate, reasonable facts. Don't be timid or hesitant, but put yourself forward frankly. In this way, you shall be honored and respected and reputed to be a valorous man, and you shall be feared so that you shall receive no insult from anyone, and shall fully receive your just due.

Once you have won your friends and relatives (I mean, once you see that they love you and serve you and care about you), you must be sensible enough to keep their friendship, and even to increase it; and this is how to do it. Don't be ungrateful for favors received; offer your own property and yourself, serve others, frequent them, honor them. Rejoice with your friends during their good times, and in times of adversity commiserate with them and show them that you are pained for them; comfort and help them, offering to do whatever is necessary. If you see that you can be useful to them or honor them, do so; don't wait to be asked. But when you've done so, or rather before, tell them so, so that with your help the favor or honor will be attained, and they shall see that you neglected nothing. In this way and others like it, as occur every day, you can win friends and keep the ones you already have, or rather add to them.

But above all, if you wish to have friends and relationships, make sure that you don't need them. Strive always to have cash and to keep it carefully; that's the best friend or relative you can have. Endeavor to attain a little status; be open — you are intelligent enough to know how to comport yourself and to do what you have been taught. Keep in mind these verses taught by our authors for our training, as you shall find in Aesop, I believe:

Tempore felici multi nominantur amici
Dum Fortuna perit nullus amicus erit.[14]

In your studies, you shall find many more true teachings like this one. By God, don't ever give up studying, but keep it up until the end of your life; for you shall derive much pleasure, much benefit, and much good advice from it. And these teachings are such that, if you know how to appreciate them, everything else will seem to you futile and useless, and you shall derive good from them in proportion to how much you follow them.

You can also learn other things, to wit: if in your city, or rather in your district or neighborhood, one or more factions should be

---

14. A medieval distich based on Ovid: "Donec eris felix multos numerabis amicos / Tempora si fuerint nubila solus eris" ("As long as your luck is good, you will have many friends / should your fortunes change, you will be alone") (*Tristia*, I, 9, 5-6).

formed, as happens every day, either to deal with city affairs, or because one citizen has a grudge on account of something the city did to him or for some other reason, if you want to live in peace and be no man's enemy and be loved and reputed wise and be listened to in every dispute, this is what you must do: stay in the middle and remain friends with everyone and don't speak ill of anyone nor try to please one more than the other; don't be moved by anger. If you want to complain, do so with anyone but someone from the opposing party; thus you will protect yourself from those who go around repeating things to defame others. If you hear people speaking well of one of the parties, join in, and listen to them willingly; if you hear them speaking ill of anyone, hold your tongue, or reproach whoever is speaking, if you think he will tolerate it. Never repeat anything bad said about anyone; if you think it will bring pleasure, repeat good things. Don't get involved if you aren't asked to, and then only say good things. If you see that you can go forward this way and make both parties happy, do so, and do so for the better; if you see that it's no use, either because of a grudge someone has against you or because you are reluctant to do what is asked of you, or because there is no faithful friend to support you, or because the two parties want to put their own friends forward, then hold back, if it is of no benefit to yourself. Then you can turn your coat. Observe which of the two parties is stronger, which is more reasonable, which has more credibility with the powers that be, which has more noble men and more Guelphs; associate yourself with that party, honor it, support it in word and deed. Be strong, and don't let yourself be dissuaded.

Keep to the straight path; don't be led astray by promises or anything else; if you did, you would be reputed disloyal, indecisive, and unstable. Nevertheless, you should always try to reason with everyone; if it is necessary to use different words, even unreasonable ones, to further your cause, do so, but let the outcome be reasonable. Don't be swayed unless you see that everyone is concurring in a case of great importance in favor of your party or your situation. You should concur, too, then, for otherwise you would be held to be suspicious and people would reject you.

Giovanni di Pagolo Morelli

You should also try to frequent one or two valorous men, wise, older, and uncorrupted; study their manners, their words, their advice, how they run their families and their households. Learn from, and try to emulate them. Always keep them foremost in your mind, and when you do anything, imagine what they would do in your place. If you speak in public or in an official capacity, keep this kind of man in your mind's eye; take heart from his example and follow his style. If you do so, you will take on his ways and won't become discouraged and will be forthright and confident, for you shall always be encouraged by his image.

And just as you can take a living man as your model, likewise or a little less you can you can take as an example a valiant Roman or some other valorous man whom you have studied. But it is not possible to imitate men like these as you can men whom you see with your own eyes, and especially in the things with which we have to deal, which are more material than those of the great events of Rome. Except that, if you should reach the highest level [of the State], then I would I advise you to strive to resemble our Roman forefathers, for as we are descended from them in essence, we should show this in virtue and substance as well.

The Epidemic of '63

There was a deadly plague in Florence in the year 1363; many people died, but the total didn't reach a fourth of what it had been in '48, when it was three times worse. In that epidemic, as I have recorded earlier, three of our father Pagolo di Bartolomeo's brothers died: Giovanni, Dino, and Calandro. The day and time of their death are written above.

The War with the Pisans

During this same year the war with the Pisans began, and it was bitter and harmful for both us and for them.[15] If the Visconti hadn't helped the Pisans, the wars would have been quickly resolved. But the house of Visconti was always the enemy of the Florentines and of all Guelphs, and friends of the Pisans and all of the Ghibellines in Tuscany.[16] During this war, the white company of the English came to Tuscany; they were the noblest company of soldiers that had ever been seen at the time, and the richest. They wanted to be hired as mercenaries for the Florentines, and showed that they were more willing to fight for us than for the Pisans. The Florentines deliberated about hiring them; and the story goes that the City would have hired them if it hadn't been for Messire Nicolò degli Alberti, who was then Stardard-bearer of Justice and wouldn't allow them to be hired on account of the great expense, to which we were not then accustomed. Thus it came about that the Pisans hired the English with the help of Messire Bernabò Visconti, the Duke of Milan, who lent them a hundred thousand florins. With the English mercenaries, the Pisans had the better of the war at the beginning, and they sacked the Florentine countryside at will and wreaked great havoc, setting fires, stealing crops, robbing people, and taking prisoners and livestock. The captain of this company of soldiers was named Andrea Belmonte; he dressed in white and was an extremely handsome young man.[17] They had sixteen thousand men. When our State saw that we had been both injured and shamed by the Pisans, our citizens attempted to recapture our honor by hiring part of that company of Englishmen. At the same time, we sent to

---

15. This war — one of many between Florence and Pisa — took place between 1362 and 1364, but it had really begun six years earlier.

16. The Visconti of Milan were natural, eternal enemies of the Florentines, for territorial reasons and on account of Florence's alliance with Genoa against Pisa.

17. Andrea Belmonte or Beaumont, an English soldier of fortune who joined the "White Company" of mercenaries that formed after the Treaty of Brétigny in 1359.

Giovanni di Pagolo Morelli

Germany and hired a fine company of lords and gentlemen, which included Count Arrigo di Monforte and Count Menno, two exceedingly valiant men, and two other counts; in all, they had two thousand horses, at the request of Francesco da Carrara, Lord of Padua. In the end, the Pisans were bitterly defeated.

One day (the day that the race of St. Victor is run[18]), after our captain, Galeotto Malatesta, had hurled every insult in the world at the city gates of Pisa, our troops went back and made camp about six miles from that city.

The weather was terribly hot that day; around the ninth hour, our soldiers, believing that they were safe, all put down their arms and removed the saddles from their horses and took their ease and refreshment in the Arno River, bathing and splashing about. The Pisans got word of this, and their captain, with all their soldiers on foot and on horseback, and the whole population of Pisa, even women armed with ropes, emerged from the city to assault our men on the battlefield; they were certain that they would win, and take everyone prisoner. But it pleased God that the opposite should happen: before the Pisans were able to reach them, they raised a great cloud of dust in the air, which made the Florentine captain suspicious. He ordered all his men to take up their arms again, just before the Pisans attacked. Our men weren't totally armed yet, and because it was toward evening, they had the sun in their eyes and the Pisans at their backs; but, as God willed it, there was a group of Genoese crossbow archers at the barricades, some of the best in the world. You could see hundreds of arrows flying through the air; and they put up such a resistance that one of the companies of British and German mercenary soldiers were able to arm themselves. The first to emerge was Count Menno, who became angry when he reached the barricades and couldn't pass, and said: "What is this?" "These are the barricades," was the answer. He said: "Open the barricades for Count Menno!" and burst forth like a paladin against the Pisans and made the fiercest attack against them that was ever seen. Between him and a few others and the crossbow archers,

---

18. July 28.

they managed to hold off the Pisans until the entire Florentine army was armed again, and they were on top of the Pisans, who were tired out from coming there in the great heat and dust. The Pisans who were on foot could barely stay standing up, and those on horseback had their weapons all hot and untempered, and their horses were so sweaty they couldn't go on. The skirmish lasted about three hours, and was bitter and cruel. While the fighting was going on, an eagle, one of the ones that the Pisans kept as symbols or mascots, flew out over the battlefield; when it was above our men, its wings seemed to give out. It fell, and was captured by our men. The Florentines were overjoyed at this omen, and the Pisans were appalled. In the end, the Pisans were routed and defeated by the Florentines, and more than fifteen hundred were killed or taken prisoner. Our citizens believed that if our captain had persevered, that day we would have conquered Pisa; but he did not choose to follow up that victory, and it was believed that he acted thus so that the Florentines would not become too powerful.

However it went, the victory was great. The Pisans who had been captured were bound with their own ropes and loaded onto fifty of their own carts; and in the first cart their eagle was hung, but not so that it would die, because its feet could reach the cart, and it was struggling violently. Their captain went in front, a prisoner, disgraced and humiliated. His name was Rinieri del Busso; he remained a prisoner for a long time in the Stinche.[19] At the gate at San Frediano, through which the captain entered, there was a little live lion cub,[20] and all the Pisan prisoners were forced to kiss its arse. And he was taken all around Florence, so that everyone, great and small, could see.

---

19. The famous Florentine prison at San Simeone. According to Villani (VIII, 75), the name came from that of a rebellious castle in the Val di Grieve, whose soldiers were the first prisoners.

20. The *marzocco*, symbol of Florence.

Giovanni di Pagolo Morelli

How the Count of Vertus Betrayed Messire Bernabò, Put Him in Prison, and Had Him Killed

At this time — that is, around 1388 or so — the Count of Vertus[21] traitorously invited Messire Bernabò to a banquet he was giving. Bernabò started off for the banquet, all unsuspectingly, and the Count started out with more than five hundred armed men on horseback. A man they called Medicina told Messire Bernabò: "Sire, take care, for the Count has more than five hundred horsemen with him and is coming to take you to prison." Bernabò laughed and said: "It can't be true; but the Count is a self-important man, so he comes here in this way." They met on the road; the Count came up to Bernabò and greeted him warmly. Then some men came up to where the Count and Bernabò were and said: "Sire, you are the prisoner of the Count of Vertus!" Disturbed, Bernabò said: "My son, why are you doing this to me? I have only your good at heart, and everything I have is yours. Don't do what no one in our family has ever done, and become a traitor!" The Count replied: "You must go to prison, because you have tried to have me killed several times." And he took him to Pavia and put him in the castle there and had him well guarded until he could take control of everything; then he had him poisoned. Messire Bernabò was the Count's uncle as well as his father-in-law; the Count was truly an evil man to do something like this. He dressed like a Franciscan monk, carried a rosary, and acted very benevolent toward his men, all with the aim of ingratiating himself with Messire Bernabò's people. But he also showed great friendship toward Bernabò's enemies, especially in Florence. Thus he was able easily to take over everything that had been his. Bernabò's sons tried to flee, but the Count had them captured and imprisoned.

---

21. The first wife of Gian Galeazzo Visconti (1351–1402) was Isabelle of France, the daughter of John the Good; the county of Vertus was part of her dowry. Bernabò died in 1385, in the castle of Trezzo d'Adda.

There was great rejoicing in Florence, for Messire Bernabò was our enemy. But certain wise men said: "We're rejoicing about our own misfortune, for one of these men is as bad as the other, and they are both our enemies." Then the Count maliciously plotted to get the lords of Padua and of Verona to make war against one another, pretending to give his support to each of them.[22] Finally, when they were both worn down and battered, he attacked them, first capturing Verona and then Padua. Shortly afterward, he had a son, and sent word to Florence that he wanted him to be baptized; the Florentine government sent Messire Maso degli Albizzi,[23] and had the child baptized; he was named Giovanni Maria. Then the Count formed a league with Florence, Siena, and Perugia.

Then, after amassing an army and preparing himself well for battle, in 1390 the Count turned on us, and waged war against us continuously for two years. During that time, the 13,000 florins in capital that Morello and I had between us got eaten into, between money we had to pay out for forced loans, interest, and land and titles to public loans that we were forced to sell. Florence spent a great deal on this war, but the Count spent two million florins. We always fought our enemy in Lombardy, keeping camps in Siena and Pisa. We had the Duke of Bavaria come as a mercenary captain with more than five thousand horses, and paid him more than a hundred thousand florins. But then he betrayed us and left with the money. Then we called in the Count of Armagnac with more than ten thousand horses, and because of his mad folly he was routed by Filippo da Pisa and Antonio Balestracci and others the moment he arrived in the city of Alessandria in Piedmont;[24] and the Florentine state paid him two

---

22. Francesco da Carrara was lord of Padua, and Antonio della Scala was lord of Verona. Verona fell to Visconti on October 17, 1387; after the armistice of November 21, 1388, Padua was ruled by a Visconti lord, Jacopo del Verme, who took power on December 18.

23. Maso degli Albizzi was a strong personality who, with Niccolò da Uzzano and Gino Capponi, dominated Florentine politics for a quarter of a century.

24. This famous battle took place on July 25, 1391; the Gascon mercenary soldiers led by Jean d'Armagnac in the service of Florence were routed by the tactics of Jacopo del Verme, as Ariosto wrote in *Orlando Furioso* XXXIII, 22).

hundred thousand florins or more. If one of these two mercenary captains had fought full force, the Duke would have been undone. Padua was won back in this war.[25]

Peace was made in 1392, thanks to the grand master of Rhodes[26] and the Genoese; the treaty was signed in Genoa. Wise men believe (and this has been amply borne out by experience) that if peace had not been made then and the war had continued even for a few more months, we would have totally undone Gian Galeazzo, because he was worn out and had no money and all of his men were furious with him. They had been promised a great deal of money, but he couldn't pay them; so they would have been forced to leave him and we could have had them at a good price. After this war, in which he accomplished great things, Sir John Hawkwood died on March 17, 1394.[27]

How the Citadel Was Lost

On the sixth day of September, the Pisans scaled the walls of the citadel and entered through a tiny door into a tower that was supposed to be guarded by an officer and eighteen mercenary soldiers. Once they had entered the tower, they climbed up, and meeting no resistance, took the towers. Then they descended using our own ladders, which were leaning against the walls; they captured every man there.

Siepe, out of great fear, cast the banners of Florence down into the moat, and opened the door for them; for after they had all

---

25. That is, it was freed from the Visconti domination by Francesco da Carrara, on June 21, 1390 (the peace treaty was concluded in January 1392).

26. The grand master of the Knights of Rhodes (also known as the Knights of Malta), the famous religious order of knights dating to the time of the Crusades.

27. The great English soldier of fortune, whom the Italians called Giovanni Acuto, is the subject of the equestrian monument painted by Paolo Uccello in Florence Cathedral in 1436.

entered into the towers as I have described, they didn't dare to descend until they saw the door open and the people come in. Rafacane opened the outer emergency door and fled headlong with all of our men. The mercenary soldiers assigned to defend the battlements had quickly arrived, and when they saw our men emerging from the citadel, they started to flee; but Rafacane and the others cried out: "We are your prisoners!" They did this in order not to fall into the hands of the Pisans; for when they had been standing guard at the citadel, all they had done was insult the Pisans and show them their arse. On top of this, they had tried to rob the infantrymen who were inside, so that many of them left. These are the precautions that these captains had taken: they had hunted for quail and sent for flasks of wine and robbed the infantrymen and insulted the Pisans and their women. The citadel was lost on Sunday, September 6. Messire Andrea came to offer aid to the Florentines at the second hour of the night; everything had been lost except one tower, and this they could barely hold. But they wouldn't surrender until Messire Andrea said that he could do nothing to help them until daylight. Then they surrendered.

The news reached Florence on the 7th of September 1405, the vigil of the feast of Our Lady; and the news was as gloomy and unpleasant as you can imagine. All true Florentines were saddened by this loss and never forgot it, on account of Florence's honor. And it shall never be forgotten, unless the proper revenge is taken, and that shall be the taking of Pisa. Then we shall believe that God has permitted this to happen for the greater honor of Florence, though we have had to toil and pay for our sins.

The Illness of My Eldest Son Alberto

During these dark, unpleasant times for me, on account of the heavy, complicated burdens I have always had to bear, on Monday morning the 19th of May, 1406, my eldest son Alberto was taken ill, with blood flowing out of his nose. He had had three nosebleeds the previous day and night, before we realized that he had a fever. On Monday morning while he was at school, the fever seized him, blood flowed out of his nose, and he lost control of his bowels. It pleased God for him to live sixteen days, in great pain and suffering until Friday night, June 5, at the third hour. His illness took this course: he continuously had a fever, which would get higher every evening; he grew worse day after day. After two days, during which he hadn't been able to keep anything in his stomach, he got a pain below his liver, above where the thigh joins the body. The pain was dangerous and excruciating, and for sixteen days he got no relief, nor did those who were caring for him; he cried out in pain continuously. His body was swollen, and he seemed in a paroxysm of pain. There is no heart so hard that wouldn't have felt pity for him, seeing him in so much pain. He beseeched God and the Virgin Mary many times, asking that the painting of Our Lady be brought before him; he embraced it with innumerable supplications, prayers, and vows, so that no one could be so hardhearted as to not be moved to great pity at the sight of him. He adjured his father, his mother, his relatives and whoever was present, with such humility and such moving words that it was astounding. At last he died; all the help we tried to give him, all our prayers and supplications and vows were of no avail; God wanted his life to come to an end!

May it please God to have brought to an end the strife, toil, and tribulation that to my mind followed my son from the time he was a little child. Of his own volition, at the age of four he wanted to come into my shop; at six, he knew the Psalms; at eight, the rudiments of Latin grammar. He knew how to write, and sent letters in his own hand to his cousins or mother when they were in the country. At nine years of age, he read the Latin authors and learned to read business letters. He had a good memory, spoke well, and could retain what he had learned; he had a pleasing appearance, and was gentle and well-mannered. He liked to take risks, and was a little wild. The death of this child was an incalculable loss to his father and mother; it saddened his relatives and neighbors, his teacher, his fellow students, the peasants at our home in the country, our servants, and anyone who had ever known or seen him. His body was laid to rest on Friday, June 5, at the 11th hour, in the church of Santa Croce, in our family sepulchre, in the passage where the men are buried; it was not out of order to give him this honor. May God give his soul repose in Heaven, and may it please Him to give life to Alberto's father, mother, brothers, and sisters, if that should be best for their souls; if not, may God do His holy will.

I could never have imagined that God taking my son from me, passing from this life to the next, could have been and continues to be such a knife in my heart. Many months have passed since the time of his death, and neither his mother nor I can forget. We continuously have his image in front of us, all his ways, the things he said and the things he did reminding us day and night, at breakfast, at supper, in the house, outside, sleeping, waking, in the country, in Florence. In any way we think about him, it keeps a knife in our hearts. And truly, this is not happening because we are obsessed with him; it's just the opposite. From the day he left us, we have tried to keep him out of our thoughts as much as possible, except when we are praying. After he died, we left the house and stayed away a month before any of us returned; and then for the entire summer no one slept in his room; and for more than a year after he died, I, Giovanni, didn't enter his room, for no other reason than overwhelming grief. May God grant that this shall not be a reason for hastening the end of our lives!

I made the sign of the cross, and settled down to go to sleep . . . But the Devil, as if he wished to recall to my mind many things in great detail and with efficacious arguments, began thus to represent to me: "Giovanni, you are completely abandoned by good fortune; you never were, nor will you ever be, entirely content in this world. You can see very well that this is true, but so that you shall be very clear about this, I shall begin at the beginning. You were born, and it was fated that you should be your father's last child to survive, which was no small misfortune.[28] Then, when you were three years old, you were left without a father, and when you were four you were abandoned by a cruel mother. During this time, you were deprived of a large part of your rightful inheritance, which had been acquired by your father through toil and industry. When you were five years old, you were given over to the care and toil of the world — that is, to school; for many years you had to study, submit to the teacher, be beaten and terrorized. In addition to this submission and torment, in your sixth year you were doubly afflicted by the harshness of the City of Florence, and from all sides and in all ways and by many people you were unjustly robbed of your property and sustenance. In your sixth year, you had a serious, long illness, which denied you the pleasures of childhood. In your eighth year, you had a teacher at home, and were subjected day and night to his discipline which, though beneficial, was unpleasant for a child's freedom. In your ninth year, you were plagued by illness and had two bouts of smallpox; the second brought you to the brink of death. Your tenth and eleventh years passed under the supervision of the teacher, which it seems to me was much harsher than is usual nowadays. In your twelfth year, you were taken to Romagna, and then to Friuli, under the superintendence of Simone Ispini, to the great disadvantage of yourself and your brothers and sisters. In Friuli you were taken ill and seriously affected by fevers, and remained for some time ill and unhappy. Finally, when you recovered, and had survived the fatal epidemic that occurred that year, the man who was a second father to you, Matteo di More Quaratesi, was taken away from you. He had treated you and your brothers and sisters like his own children, and cared for you devotedly. At his death, you lost half of what was rightfully yours and all of what had been his, which he had left to you as if you were his own children. You were saddened by the loss of this inheritance of which you defenseless children had been deprived, not so much for its value, but rather for the delightful country

---

28. After the birth of Giovanni, Pagolo Morelli had a fifth child, who died immediately.

house in which you had been raised in happier times. And where you used to take pleasure in the countryside, now that your fortunes had changed, you began to dislike it.

If you consider well, you were at an age that should be the most pleasurable, but you were already beset by worries about your affairs. Your spirit was oppressed by constantly hearing how badly things were going for you; you wanted to take some action to set things right, and your powerlessness caused you much torment. This continued for several years, and still does to this day, but with less affliction now that the years have taught you how to understand and deal with suffering. From the time you were fifteen to twenty years of age, you had not a moment's rest, and were continually beset by misfortunes. Your eldest sister, who was married, died, and you had to find a husband for your other sister; you had to make several loans of money to the State (the war with the Duke of Milan had begun); you were beset by your in-laws and neighbors, who begrudged you what you had; and you contracted a horrible illness that lasted a year; you were sick of yourself, sick of those who cared for you, sick of everyone you knew.

When you had recovered from this illness, you contacted an even worse one, but you didn't realize it: you fell head over heels in love with a woman who caused you much torment and deprived you of much good and honor, and you lost a great deal of time on account of her. Finally, she was promised to you in marriage as you desired, and just to make you suffer more, her family reneged on the agreement and she was given to another man. You were devastated by this, not realizing that you were fortunate it had happened. In your twenty-first year, you had to struggle with forced loans and reparations; you had to sell your best property. You lived in this hell, having to change your residence several times, until your thirty-fifth year. And your bad luck still continues. You have lost your position in the State, you have lost out on account of your evil relations, you are without money, without allies, without State honors; you can see no way you'll ever have them, and you have no one to comfort and assist you.[29] You are

---

29. See note 14 above.

related by marriage to people who can hurt you rather than help you.[30] You rejected those who could have helped you and brought you honor. You haven't enjoyed a penny of the inheritance left you by your father; it has brought you sorrow, not pleasure. You have had sixteen serious illnesses in your life; you've never had a piece of good news in your life, and if you did, it only brought you sorrow.

The best news you ever had was when your wife had your first child, and this was turned into the greatest sorrow and the greatest torment you ever had. Your first child was a son, so that his death would really break your heart. You saw him intelligent and healthy, so when you lost him you would suffer more; you loved him and yet you never gave him any of your wealth. You didn't treat him like a son, but like a stranger; you never gave him a moment's rest; you never looked on him kindly; you never kissed him once; you worked him to death in your shop, and thrashed him cruelly and often. And finally, when he was mortally ill, you didn't realize that he was on the brink of death and so you didn't let him make his peace with God (though as young as he was, God surely had already pardoned him), so that his soul and yours might be comforted. You watched him die in excruciating pain and torment, and never saw him have a moment's respite for the sixteen days that his illness lasted. You have lost him, and you shall never see him again in this world; and the memory of his death will make you always go in fear and torment for your other children."

Pondering upon and remembering these things and many other sad, painful memories, I became desperate almost to the point of putting an end to all those adversities. But then I turned to the Crucifix and commended myself to Christ and meditated upon His sufferings, which were infinite; and I took comfort in realizing that my own sufferings were nothing compared to the bitter Passion of Christ. I realized that I wasn't alone, for almost everyone is afflicted in one way or another. Thus, having found relief for my soul, I fell asleep.

---

30. i.e., the Alberti family.

Bonaccorso Pitti

Ricordi

In 1375, being young, inexperienced, and eager to see the world and seek my fortune, I joined up with Matteo dello Scelto Tinghi,[1] who was a merchant and also a great gambler. We went to Genoa, Pavia, back to Genoa, and on to Nice and then Avignon. While we were there during the Christmas holidays, we were seized by the Pope's marshal and thrown into prison. After we had been in prison for eight days, we were interrogated; they said we were spies for the Florentine government. They produced a letter to Matteo from his brother in Florence, saying that Bologna had rebelled against the Pope at the instigation of the Florentines and with their assistance. After many questions and answers, the court realized that we were innocent of the charge. Nonetheless, they demanded that we pay 3,000 florins in bail to prevent us from leaving Avignon without the permission of the Pope's marshal. Matteo found someone to put up the bail, and once we were out of prison he wisely decided that it was very dangerous for us to stay there on account of the

---

1. Tinghi was one of the leaders of an anti-government group in 1381, but later carried out several missions for the Florentine Republic. He was a powerful ally of the Albizzi family.

war that our city was waging in the Papal States.² He decided we should leave, with the intention of reimbursing the merchants who had stood our bail if they should be forced to pay. We left, returning to Florence as quickly as we could; and we hadn't been there long when letters came from Avignon with the news that that the Pope had imprisoned all the Florentines there, and seized all their records and goods. We heard the same from everywhere in Western Europe, where people were being arrested and their property seized on account of Pope Gregory's decree against all Florentines. But for all that, our city did not cease to wage war against the evil clerics of that time; for that matter, I never saw a good priest before or since.

The next year, Matteo decided to go to Prussia³ and to take me with him. He sent me on ahead, telling me to wait for him in Padua or Venice, where he would join me within a month. I visited Padua, Vicenza, and Verona and then came back to Padua, whence I left for Venice. Matteo came, and bought a thousand ducats worth of saffron. From Venice we set sail for Sena in Slavonia and then made our way by land to Zagreb and Buda,⁴ where Matteo sold the saffron at 1,000 ducats' profit. Because I had fallen seriously ill with a fever and two swollen glands in the groin, Matteo left me in Buda at the home of Michele Marucci,⁵ and left Michele 12 ducats for my passage back to Florence, if I should survive. And he promised that whatever Michele spent on my illness he would repay upon his return. He went on his way, leaving me alone and very ill cared for. My bed was a large sack of straw in a warming room;⁶ no doctor ever came to visit me, and there were no women in the

---

2. The war between Florence and Pope Gregory XI (1370–1378) was called the War of the Eight Saints after the "Otto di Guerra," the committee that presided over Florence's military activities.

3. This name was generally used to denote the northern part of Germany, then dominated by the Teutonic Order.

4. Buda was then separate from Pest, with which it would later form Budapest.

5. A Florentine merchant and speculator who acted as Tinghi's agent.

6. A *stufa secca*, a room warmed by hot air coming from below or the sides (mentioned in *Decameron* day II, tale 4).

house — only a servant boy who cooked and served Michele and two merchants who were staying with him. I was on the brink of death. After lying in that room for six whole weeks, on the night of St. Martin a party of Germans gathered to play the pipes and dance in a large room across from the where I lay on the sack of straw with a towel instead of a sheet under me and a shaggy blanket and my greasy fur coat over me. They stuck their heads in to see who was there, and finding me, forced me into my fur coat and dragged me around and around the room, saying to me: "Either you'll get better or you'll die and then you won't have to suffer any longer." They dragged me around the room for the better part of an hour in spite of all my entreaties, and only let go of me when I collapsed from exhaustion. Then they put me back on my sack, threw their lined cloaks on top of me, and went back to their drinking and dancing. They kept it up all night while I sweated under that pile of clothes. In the morning when they came for their cloaks, they forced me to dress again and to have a drink with them, which I did willingly enough. They left, and I rested for perhaps an hour and then went out to the home of Bartolomeo di Guido Baldi of Florence, who was master of the royal mint at Buda. He was happy to see me, and kept me to dine with him; after we had dined, we started to gamble. With 55 Venetian *soldini*, which was all the money I had left, I won 4 florins from him. At that moment there arrived several Jews and some more Germans, who used to come often to gamble with Bartolomeo. They began to gamble and I with them, and at the end of the day I brought home 20 gold florins that I had won. The next day I returned and won about 40 gold florins, and so on every day for 15 whole days, by which time I found I had won 1,200 florins or thereabouts with my 55 *soldini*. Michele Mariucci kept begging me to stop gambling, saying, "Buy some horses[7] and go back to Florence, and I will go with you as far as Segna, for I'm leaving for there in a few days." In fact, I took his advice and bought six fine horses

---

7. The market for horses in Hungary was very favorable at this time. See *Venezia e Ungheria nel Rinascimento* (Florence, 1973), pp. 145 ff.

and hired a page and four servants. When we reached Segna, Michele sold me five of his own horses. I hired a boat from Marseilles and loaded the horses on it; but there was a storm and the winds were against us, so I barely reached Venice in 24 days. And while we were unloading the horses one of the best of them put its shoulder out. When we reached Padua, I gave one of the horses to Giorgio Bagnesi, who was living there with his wife, Madonna Caterina, a daughter of Niccolò Malegonelle and a cousin of mine. I left Padua for Florence and took the Modena road on account of the war that the Bolognese were waging;[8] in the mountains above Modena another good horse was ruined, and I left it at Pontremoli. I made it back to Florence with 8 horses, six of which I sold, and lost all of the money gambling. Indeed, six months later, between losses and money spent on clothes and other expenses, I was left with no more than about a hundred florins and two horses.

While I was in these straits, I fell in love with a woman named Madonna Gemma, the widow of Jacopo, the son of Messire Rinieri Cavicciuli, and the daughter of Giovanni Tedaldini. She was staying in a convent outside the city gates at Pinti, and I happened to be passing by one day and some of her relatives invited me in for refreshments; I accepted. Although there were many people present, I managed to speak to her privately, and said to her respectfully: "I am all yours; I commend myself to you." "If you are mine, would you obey me if I gave you a command?" she replied, laughing. Said I: "Try me." She replied: "Go to Rome for love of me."[9] I went home and two days later set out with a servant, without telling them at home where I was going. I went to Siena and thence to Perugia, Todi, Spoleto, Terni, Narni, and Orte, where the Florentine league was fighting the Romans.[10] I begged Messire Bindo Bondelmonti to accompany me to Rome

---

8. A consequence of the War of the Eight Saints, because Bologna was part of the Papal States and was governed by a papal legate.

9. This was a ploy that ladies used to rid themselves of importunate lovers, reminiscent of certain episodes in the *Decameron* (day IX, tale 1; day X, tale 5).

10. Again, this was part of the War of the Eight Saints.

one night with some of his men; he smuggled me into the house of a Roman who was a secret friend of his, where I stayed for several days. This Roman, whose name was Cola Ciencio,[11] got me a safe-conduct pass for eight days. When I had been there for six days, Cola had me taken to an estate that belonged to the Orsini,[12] and from there to Orte, whence I returned to Florence by the way I had come. Between going and staying and coming back from Rome, I was gone for a month. When I returned, I sent a woman to tell Madonna Gemma how I had obeyed her. She sent back word that she had never supposed that I would be so foolish as to take such a risk for something she had said in jest. This was in 1377.

Turmoil Among the Populace, Voluntary Exile and Conspiracies

In 1378, after peace had been made with Pope Gregory,[13] turmoil broke out among the Florentine populace.[14] The unskilled workers burned and sacked a number of houses and drove the Priors from the Public Palace and with them Luigi Guicciardini, who was Standard-bearer of Justice at the time. They then proceeded to seize power and to appoint a Standard-bearer of their own choosing, a certain Michele di Lando, who, however, made common cause with the artisans, the Ghibellines, and men barred from office, and drove the populace out of power. As a militiaman under the Nicchio standard,[15] I was on duty in the square when the artisans and their allies were returning after the mob had been expelled from the Public Palace. When all the others

---

11. Perhaps a member of the noble Cenci family.
12. The Orsini were a prominent Roman family who were traditionally friendly to the Florentines and their merchants, and enemies of Pope Gregory XI.
13. This is one of Pitti's rare mistakes; Gregory XI died in March of 1378, and peace was made with his successor, Urban VI, in July of that year.
14. Pitti is referring to the so-called Ciompi Rebellion in July of 1378.
15. One of the four subdivisions of the civil militia in the Santo Spirito quarter.

had quieted down, a stonecutter, who was clearly in a murderous mood, kept shouting "Death to them! Death to them!" I walked over and told him to hold his tongue, whereupon he lunged at my chest with the point of his sword. I quickly drew a spear on him and, running it through his leather tunic, killed him on the spot. Several witnesses who had seen him start the trouble declared that I had acted in self-defense and that he deserved what he got. No more was said about it at the time.

I went home; and seeing that many Guelf citizens, and some of the best, were being driven out and banished, I decided not to stay in Florence. I went to Pisa, where I was joined by Matteo Tinghi, who had been exiled. After I had been there for several months, we heard that a number of Guelf citizens were planning to start an insurrection in Florence with the help of a band of proscribed men, who were to come from Siena under the leadership of Messire Luca, the son of Totto da Panzano. When they heard this, Giovanni dello Scelto Tinghi and Bernardo di Lippo organized and headed a contingent from Pisa of some 200 exiles, proscribed men, and sympathizers. I joined this group and, according to plan, went with them one night to the gate of San Piero Gattolino.[16] Messire Luca's men were supposed to reach San Miniato al Monte late the same night so as to give the signal at dawn. This was to be a signal for the conspirators in Florence to arm themselves, take to the streets, and open the gate of San Giorgio to us.[17] Accordingly, our party sent to find out whether Messire Luca was at San Miniato. He was not, for the plot in the city had been discovered, and Messire Gregorio Tornaquinci had been arrested along with several others, from whom the city authorities learned of Messire Luca's plan to come in from Santa Maria Impruneta with his men.[18] The Defender[19] was promptly sent out with a number of foot soldiers and sixty cavalrymen who, coming upon Messire Luca's

---

16. The modern-day Porta Romana.

17. The exiles were approaching Florence from the South, as indicated by the places named.

18. About a dozen kilometers from Florence, Santa Maria Impruneta had been famous since the early fourteenth century for its miraculous Madonna, its artisans, and its fair.

party, captured seven and routed the rest. Knowing nothing of this, and hearing that Messire Luca was not at the appointed place, our group thought we must have come a day too soon. Accordingly, we retreated from Florence towards Pozzolatico,[20] split into small group, and sought refuge in the houses of friends. I went with Giovanni Tinghi and Gerardo di Lippo to Giovanni Corbizi's house in Pozzolatico, where we found shelter for ourselves, six horses, and twelve foot soldiers. Around three in the afternoon, a number of fugitives from Florence arrived with the news that Messire Gregorio had been arrested and that the whole city was under martial law. We were still convinced that we had arrived a day early, and hopeful that Messire Luca might still turn up the next night with his men. As soon as evening came, I mounted my horse and set off for Santa Maria Impruneta with two comrades, who were on foot, to see if I could get any news of Messire Luca. At about one in the morning I ran into the Defender, who had the seven men from Messire Luca's party who had been captured. Believing that this was Messire Luca's contingent, I happily joined them, but we were immediately surrounded by men pointing their lances at us and saying "Who are you?" Realizing the fix I was in, I boldly replied: "Friends." A mounted mace-bearer came forward and asked me: "What's your name?" I said: "I'm Bonaccorso." Then he told the foot soldiers: "Let him go, he's a friend." By this time they were all around me, and the path was so narrow and rough that I could see no way of turning back. I pressed forward until I came to where the Defender was with the men on horseback; he stopped and asked me: "Who are you?" "I am Bonaccorso Pitti," I boldly replied, "the mace-bearer back there recognized me at once." "What are you doing at this hour, armed like this?" he asked me; for I was wearing a cuirass and had a lance in my hand, and my comrades had lances on their shoulders. "I have a quarrel with someone; I left Florence when they closed the city gates

---

19. *Il Difensore* was a police functionary brought from another city to keep order in Florence, also against political conspirators.

20. About 7 kilometers from Florence, near the confluence of the Ema and Greve rivers.

and I'm on my way to San Casciano. I took this road for fear of being ambushed; I was also glad to take it because I knew you were in Santa Maria Impruneta." "I believe you," he said, "but just in case you might be one of the men I'm searching for, I want you to come back to Florence with me." Said I: "I am very happy to do so," and turned my horse around. Then he asked my name again; I told him, and he questioned me again. I gave him the same answers, without kowtowing to him in the least. Then he said: "It doesn't seem right to me to make you turn back, yet I am afraid of being blamed if I let you go." I boldly replied: "Your Honor," don't worry about inconveniencing me, for I am very happy to return with you." Then he said: "Go with God." I left him, riding on; when I was out of sight of his men, I turned another way, and returned to the comrades I had left behind and told them what had befallen me. We resolved to lie low until daybreak, when I led them by back roads to Sorbigliano by way of Mezzola, where Messire Zanobi kept us to dine. After I had led them in safety to the road to Siena, I left them and returned to Pisa. All the roads were being guarded and I was in constant danger of being captured. But I didn't start to get frightened until I had reached a safe place not far from Pisa. Then I was so overcome with fear and exhaustion — not having slept for three nights — that I stayed at Pontedera and rested for two days. When I got to Pisa I heard that Messire Gregorio and the seven prisoners had been beheaded, and that I had been tried *in absentia* with many others and had been sentenced to be beheaded.

Seeing the World and Seeking My Fortune

Bernardo di Lippo and I decided to go to France. We went to Rimini, where we borrowed fifty ducats from Giovanni di Masino dell'Antella, who was living there, and without tarrying we left immediately for Avignon and then Tarascon, where we visited

Messire Stoldo Altoviti and Messire Tommaso Soderini, who had been exiled from Florence. We left them and went to Paris, where we stayed only a short time, for Bernardo di Cino[21] sent me to gamble with the Duke of Brabant,[22] who was in Brussels with many great noblemen who were amusing themselves with great jousts and tournaments, dancing, and gambling. A few days after arriving in Brussels, I had already lost 2,000 gold francs[23] that belonged to Bernardo di Cino, with whom I had gone into partnership on the understanding that he was to supply the money, and I my foolish bent for gambling. I lost the money by making bets of 300 florins or more on each throw of the dice, having deluded myself that playing for high stakes would bring me greater profits. On my last night, I lost 500 francs, which I had borrowed from the Duke; since all I had at my lodging was about 550 gold francs, I left off playing.

The Duke and a group of gentlemen rose and went into another room, where many ladies and gentlemen were dancing. As I stood enjoying the spectacle, a 14-year-old girl, unmarried, the daughter of a great baron, came up to me and said: "Come and dance, Lombard;[24] don't fret over your losses, for God will surely help you." And she took me by the hand and led me onto the floor. When I had finished dancing with her, the Duke called me over and asked, "How much have you lost tonight?" I told him that I had lost all that was left of the 2,000 francs I had brought from Brussels. He said, "I believe you, though if I had lost such a sum I wouldn't be able to show a face as cheerful as yours. Go back and enjoy yourself now. It can do you nothing but good." The next morning, I brought the Duke a purse containing 500 gold francs and begged his leave to depart, explaining that I wanted to

---

21. Bernardo di Cino di Bartolino de' Benvenuti, who by a privilege granted by King Charles V of France in 1379 called himself and his family nobles.

22. Wenceslaus of Luxembourg.

23. The three types of coins mentioned here had different values, since they contained different amounts of gold: the Venetian ducat contained 3.559 grams, the franc 3.885 grams, and the florin 3.536 grams.

24. In France, Burgundy, and England, all inhabitants of the northern and central regions of Italy were called "Lombards" (see *Decameron* day I, tale 1).

seek better fortune elsewhere. He said to me, "Stay if you like, and try to recoup your losses with these 500 francs. If you lose them, you can pay me back some other time, when you're more prosperous." I thanked him, but said that I did not want to play any more for a while and that I had urgent reasons for going to England. He told me to keep the 500 francs anyway, and that I could pay him back if I ever returned and won back the money I had lost. Then he summoned one of his chancellors and told him, "Make out a letter for Bonaccorso saying that he is personally attached to my service and so on." I left Brussels and went to England; after I was there for about a month, negotiating the terms of a ransom to be paid for Jean of Brittany[25] as I had been commissioned to do by the Duke of Lancaster, in whose hands the prisoner was being held, I returned to Paris and reported to Bernardo about everything I had done in Brussels and in England.

In 1381, after I had returned to Paris, I was very short of money because of my losses in Brussels, for I was obliged to return a fourth of the 2,000 francs I had lost to Bernardo di Cino. I gave him the 500 francs that the Duke of Brabant had lent me. In February of that same year, I returned to Brussels with about 200 gold francs, which I had obtained from several people, and in Brussels I borrowed 300 francs from Bernardo da Varazzano. While I was gambling with the Duke and some other gentlemen, letters arrived from Florence with news that the exiles had returned there. I stayed in Brussels until the end of Lent, by which time I had about 600 gold francs. On my way back through Paris, I bought several fine horses; I reached Florence in the month of May 1382.

The following September, I returned to Paris; in November, on St. Catherine's day, I took part in a battle that the King of France was fighting in Flanders near Ypres against the Flemish, or rather against the men of Ghent, whose leader was Philippe van Artevelde. The Flemish had a force of 40,000 armed men;

---

25. Jean of Brittany or Jean de Blois, delivered as a hostage for his father Charles de Blois, who had been captured by the English in 1345. Jean remained a prisoner for more than thirty years; he was freed in 1387.

we, on the King's side, were 10,000 men. The battle was fought on foot, at sunrise. What seemed miraculous was that, although at first the mist was so thick it was almost like night, when the King, who had divided us into three divisions, ordered his standard-bearer to unfurl a banner that is called the oriflamme,[26] which is supposed to have been a gift of God to his ancestors, the mist melted away and the two sides were able to see each other by the light of the sun. The French commander-in-chief opened the battle by leading the first of the three French divisions against the Flemish, who were drawn up in a single formation. It was all over in two hours; the Flemish were defeated by that single French division. The order was to take no prisoners; in the end, the number of dead Flemish soldiers was 27,500. As soon as the battle was won, we moved on quickly to Courtray, a town about the size of Prato, which was taken and sacked and burned to the ground to avenge the defeat that the French had suffered near there many years before at the hands of the Flemish when, as one may read in the chronicles of Filippo Villani,[27] a great number of French knights lost their lives. After this, the King set out for Paris at the head of his victorious army.

Bonaccorso's Return to Florence; Marriage, Missions to France

I arrived in Florence and decided to take a wife. Since Guido di Messire Tommaso di Neri del Palagio was the most respected, influential man in the city, I resolved to put the matter in his hands and leave the choice of my bride up to him, provided he selected

---

26. From the Latin *aurea flamma*. This was the standard of the King of France: a banner of smooth red fabric divided into three strips, edged in green silk and hung from a gilded lance.
27. It was not Filippo, but rather Giovanni Villani who described the Battle of Courtray, which the French lost to the Flemish in 1302.

her from among his own relations. I calculated that if I were to become a connection of his and could win his good will, he would be obliged to help me obtain a truce with the Corbizzi family. Accordingly, I sent the marriage-broker, Bartolo della Contessa, to tell Guido of my intentions. He sent Bartolo back with the message that he would be happy to have me as a kinsman and was giving some thought to the matter. A few days later, he sent Bartolo a second time to say that if I liked I might have the daughter of Luca, son of Piero degli Albizzi, whose mother was a first cousin of his own. I sent back word that I would be very happy and honored and so forth. I was betrothed to her at the end of July 1391, and married her on November 12 of the same year.

I was a member of the Eight on Security;[28] one day, before I got married, I happened to be in the Public Palace with several comrades when lightening struck the palace tower and grounded not far from where I was sitting, so that the fire touched my calves. When I tried to stand up, I collapsed on the ground, paralyzed from the knees down; my legs felt like they were on fire. They removed my hose, which stank of sulfur, for the lightning had missed me by a hair. All the flesh on my legs was covered with welts; the skin was bleeding, and the hair was singed. They rubbed my legs, which were as cold as those of a dead man; thinking I was dying, I asked for a priest. Half an hour later, I stretched my legs, put on another pair of hose, and walked home on my own two feet. The wool I had bought in England arrived on two ships before my marriage. The insurance for the consignment that was unloaded in Genoa was nine percent of the cost; on the ship that came to Pisa, I paid fourteen. When the wool was sold and the money collected, I found that I had made 1,000 gold florins on the venture in sixteen months. I deposited this money with Luigi and Gherardo Canigiani, to whom I had already entrusted 4,000 gold florins, for which I accepted letters of exchange, when I arrived in Florence. This money greatly improved the credit enjoyed by the Canigiani.

---

28. This group was in charge of the police, especially for the security of the state and of the city. They also had a voice in military and fiscal affairs.

Bonaccorso Pitti

Before getting married, I spent about 2,000 gold florins on building costs and furnishings, and over the years I have had so many restorations and improvements done on this place that I have spent more than 2,500 gold florins to date just on construction and tending to vineyards and orchards.

Before I married, having decided to deal generously with that ingrate, my steward, I gave him 300 gold florins, though I only owed him 200. I also entrusted to him another 700 florins, and yielded to his request to let him go to Paris and engage in any profitable business he might find. We had agreed that for three years we would each get half of whatever money he made, and if he lost the entire 1,000 gold florins, I would repay him the 300 that I had given him. He went to Paris, where my brother Francesco got him together with our kinsman Luigi di Bartolomeo Giovanni. Since Luigi had stayed in my house and had worked for me collecting debts (I had sent him several times to Savoy, where he succeeded twice in getting 1,000 francs from the Count), I gave him 300 gold francs upon my departure from Paris. Having arranged this ill-fated partnership, Francesco left them in Paris and returned to Florence in April. I found him a wife, and he got married in June. In September he returned to Paris, taking my brother Bartolomeo with him. That December I went to Milan, taking with me Antonio Canigiani, and then I went to Pavia and to Genoa. I left on February 2nd and arrived in Florence on the 5th at 3:00 in the afternoon. In March Francesco returned to Florence, leaving Bartolomeo in Paris. He told me that Bartolomeo and my steward had lost everything, and that all that was left was our house and its furnishings, which were worth a total of 1,000 francs. Thus of the 3,000 I had left them between cash and the value of the house and its contents, they lost 2,000 francs.

In May I took horse and set out for Avignon and Paris. While I was stopping at an inn in Pavia, I happened to be leaning on the banister at the top of a flight of stairs when a servant, running down, startled a large horse that was tied to a lower part of the banister. The beast gave such a tug that it pulled down the railing to which it was tied, and the one upon which I was leaning. I fell into the yard below, hit my head against a bin of oats, and passed out. I broke no bones, and didn't bleed, but I lay there for more than two hours. When I came to, I opened my eyes and asked whether I had broken an arm or a leg. Then I felt a strong ache in my head, and on the side upon which I had fallen. I asked, "What happened? Who hit me?" For I could not, nor did I ever, remember falling. But I did remember the horse that had been frightened by the servant. The Duke of Milan sent all of his doctors to me. They drew a great deal of blood from several veins, kept me in the dark with the windows closed for nine days, gave me medicines, and applied ointments and poultices to my head. On the tenth day I got up and went to thank the Duke. I took leave of him and went to Avignon and thence to Paris, where I found Bartolomeo sick. Between expenses and gambling, he had contracted debts amounting to about 600 gold francs since Francesco's departure. I also saw the other two sorry partners in mismanagement, who told me, truly or falsely, that they had lost or spent everything. I kept my temper and restored order to my affairs. By the winter of 1393, I had repaid the 600 francs owed by Bartolomeo and given the 300 francs to the steward, as I had promised. I also satisfied Luigi and had about 500 francs left.

In September [1395] the King made a pilgrimage to Mont St. Michel in Normandy, about 150 miles from Paris; the Duke of Orleans went, too, and I with him. When we arrived, we visited the abbey, which is built on a huge rock five miles out to sea; you can reach it by land at low tide. On his way back to Paris, the King accepted the hospitality of a Norman nobleman, the Seigneur d'Hambye. The Dukes of Berry, Bourbon, and Orleans, and many other great lords and gentlemen who were travelling with the King, stayed there for a day and a night. To make things more festive for them, there were many beautiful women and great baronesses. I mention the Lord of Hambye because it was believed that he spent more than 4,000 gold francs that day in the King's honor, and it was said that this was his entire income for the year. The King brought him back to Paris and showered him with gifts of jewels, horses, and cash to the value of about 10,000 francs, so he paid well and generously for the hospitality he had received. Certainly, that feast was a marvelous and grand thing to see.

The next day after supper I accompanied the Duke of Orleans to the home of one of the King's equerries, whose name was Siferval. A number of gentlemen who had dined there were gambling when we arrived. The Duke sat down to play, and had me place on the table around 400 francs that I had brought for the two of us. It happened that when it was my turn to throw the dice, I played against the Viscount of Monlev,[29] a big gambler and a great, rich nobleman who had an annual income of more than 30,000 francs. People began to talk because I won 12 times in a row, both when I threw the dice and when he did. He had been drinking wine and had grown heated by the game, and began to say to me: "Ah, you villainous Lombard traitor, are you going to go on winning all night, you barbarous bugger?" I replied: "My lord, please speak decently, out of consideration for His Grace the Duke." He laid another bet; I won. At this he flew into a rage again, saying more foul words, and ended up with: "And I'm not lying." "Well, prove it, my lord!" I promptly replied. Then he stretched out his hand, grabbed the hat off my head, and made as if to strike me. I pulled back and said: "I'm not a man to let myself be struck when I'm armed," and put my hand upon the short rapier I wore at my side. He screamed, "I've never failed to carry out a threat, so now I'll have to kill you!" Then the Duke whispered to me to go and wait for him in his room, and leave things to him. I left; when I had gotten about a hundred yards from the house, I heard someone running up behind me. I turned around and saw, by the light of the torches of a group of courtiers who happened to be passing by at that moment, one of the bastard sons of the Viscount of Monlev with a naked dagger in his hand. I drew my rapier and said: "Bastard, sheathe your dagger and go back and tell your father you couldn't find me." He looked around, and seeing that none of his friends were coming, decided for his own good to do as I said; he sheathed his dagger and

---

29. Probably Robert de Béthune, Viscount of Meaux (Brucker).

turned back. The courtiers who had been passing told many people what had occurred, and I was greatly commended, for the bastard son was only 18 years old and was so weakly that I probably would have injured him if we had fought.

I went to the Duke's chamber, and shortly afterward he entered, greatly agitated, without saying anything to me. He said to one of his grooms: "Go to the Viscount's home and tell him that before I go to sleep I want to know whether he intends to do what I asked him." The groom went, and came back with the message that the Viscount hadn't changed his mind. Then the Duke told me: "Don't leave this house without me, for I will protect you in spite of him, and will do him little honor." The next morning we took horse and set out after the King, who had already departed. We caught up with him at an abbey where he had dismounted to take some refreshment, and the Duke told him everything that had happened the night before, and asked permission to protect his dependents, of whom I was one. The King replied, "The Viscount spoke and acted wrongly, and Bonaccorso could not fail to answer him for the sake of his honor; but I don't want this affair to go any further." Then he summoned to him the Duke of Berry and the Duke of Bourbon and several other lords, and said to them with an angry look on his face: "Send for the Viscount and tell him that before he leaves this room I want him to do as my brother wishes about the dispute he had with Bonaccorso last night." The Viscount came, and the Duke of Berry spoke to him in the presence of the King and everyone else, and told him what the King had commanded. The Viscount turned to the Duke of Orleans and said: "Sire, I am very pained that you should have taken the side of a Lombard against me, your relative and humble servant. There was no need for you to speak to the King about this, for I do not wish to disobey your orders. If I refused your request last night, I did so thinking that you weren't serious about it; but now that I see you are, I am willing to overlook the way that Bonaccorso spoke to me in your presence last night." The Duke replied, "You started things by speaking to Bonaccorso in such a way in my presence that if he had remained silent I would have thought him unworthy." I was standing nearby and had heard everything that the King and everyone else had said; I came forward and made the appropriate reverence to the Duke of Berry, who said: "His Majesty the King has heard about the words you had last night with the Viscount, and is greatly displeased. Bonaccorso, you were certainly overly bold to give the lie to such a nobleman, who is related to ourselves and who has the right to challenge and fight with any lord or prince, be they ever so great, with the sole exception of the members of the royal house of France. But since His Majesty is disposed to clemency and does not want this matter to go any further, he desires the Viscount to pardon you and that the two of you be friends as before. Therefore, Bonaccorso, beg the Viscount's pardon." I turned to the Viscount and said, "Sire, forgive me if I have said or done anything to displease you." He replied: "Since it pleases the King and my lord his brother, I would forgive you even if you had slashed my face. So I forgive you, and I also beg your pardon, and wish to be your good friend."

When we returned to Paris, I invited the Duke of Orleans and the Duke of Bourbon to dine at my house. They came, bringing with them the Sire of Coucy and the Viscount and many other barons and lords. They were so well served with viands and entremets that they spoke handsomely of them, praising me before the King and other lords. That supper cost me two hundred francs. My guests only had one complaint about me, which was that I refused to gamble that night, though there was a fine gambling session, and for high stakes; but I had invited Bernardo di Cione de' Nobili, who was the most courtly and lavish gambler ever seen.

On the 16th of January 1407, I went on an embassy to the pope[30] in Marseilles, and thence to the King and other noblemen in France, to try to obtain the release of two of Florence's ambassadors, Messire Bartolomeo Popoleschi and Bernardo Guadagni,

---

30. The Avignon anti-pope, Benedict XIII.

whom the Dukes of Orleans and Burgundy had taken hostage in reprisal for our having taken Pisa, which they said was theirs. When I arrived in Paris, I found Messire Alberto di Pepo degli Albizzi, who was living there; he had been assigned to work with me on this mission. In short, the Duke of Orleans,[31] who was keeping the two Florentines imprisoned at Blois, 3 days' ride from Paris, agreed to let the prisoners come to Paris in exchange for our word and theirs that they would not leave Paris without his permission. They came to Paris, and while their release was being negotiated, in an act of foul treachery the Duke of Burgundy had the Duke of Orleans assassinated at three in the morning on November 23, 1407.[32] Before the murder occurred, while Messire Alberto and I were at Senlis waiting upon the Duke of Orleans in hope of prevailing on him to free the prisoners, the Duke sent for me late one night. He was in a room gambling with some other noblemen; when I came in, he told me that he wished me to play with them. I replied that I had given up gambling more than eight years before, and that I hoped he would not be displeased if I didn't play, especially since I was on an official mission. But I said that once he freed the prisoners, if he still wanted me to play, I would obey him. He replied that my being on a mission was not a good excuse, as that should make me all the more eager to please him by playing. I replied that I would play to please him, but that I had only brought enough money from Florence to cover my expenses. Then he said: "Go on, sit down and play with my money," and put a large amount of gold *écus* in front of me. I began to play, and the game went in such a way that in the end I lost five hundred gold *écus* that night. Early the next morning, I rode to Paris to see if I could borrow enough money to pay back the Duke and recoup my losses. When I got to Paris the first person I asked was my ungrateful steward, who told me he couldn't

---

31. Due to the illness of Charles VI, the Duke of Orleans, who as we have seen was very close to Bonaccorso, shared the ruling of France with his great rival, the Duke of Burgundy.

32. A year later, the Duke of Burgundy would be assassinated, in the bloody struggle between the Orleans and Burgundy factions for control of France.

lend me the 200 florins I asked of him. Then I asked Bartolo di Bernardo di Cino for a hundred florins, which he lent me. I asked Luigi di Bartolomeo Giovanni for a hundred, and he lent them to me. I asked Michele de' Pazzi for 300, but he said that he had already lent them. I asked Baldo di Guido Baldi for 400, and he, too, said they were lent out. I asked Calcidonio degli Alberti for 500, and he said he didn't have cash but that he would give me a bill of exchange payable in some other place. I decided not to ask any more of my friends, but accepted a bill of exchange from Calcidonio for 500 gold florins, payable in Montpellier.[33] With that sum, and the money lent me by Bartolo and Luigi, I went to see the Duke and handed him a purse with the 500 gold *écus* I owed him. He was delighted, and commended me and so on. After dinner, the gambling began, and I won back around 200 gold *écus*. The next day, the Duke and all his retinue went to Paris. We had many more gambling sessions up to the time of the Duke's death, and I ended up about 2,000 gold *écus* to the good. After the Duke's death, Messire Bartolomeo Popoleschi and Bernardo Guadagni were freed by the Duchess and her sons and given leave to go, and they returned to Florence. I stayed on in Paris until September; then I returned to Florence on October 12, 1408 to find myself a Consul of the Wool Guild.

On October 5, 1414, I left Florence for Pisa, where I boarded one of the three galleys that had come from Provence to take Pope John to Avignon. I had them let me off at Fréjus, where I bought three pack-horses, to which I added a fourth at Avignon. At Tarascon I visited King Louis, who welcomed me warmly. On leaving him, I went to Paris by way of the Alps and Auvergne. In

---

33. Brucker observes how Bonaccorso turned to this Florentine banker working in Paris on other occasions, entering into transactions illustrated by R. de Roover, *The Rise and Decline of the Medici Bank* (Cambridge, Mass., 1963), p. 109. This type of transaction involved an advance of funds in one place and its repayment in another, usually in another currency.

Paris, I tried to collect the balance of what the Count of Savoy owed me, and to claim the estate of Luigi di Bartolomeo Giovanni, who had named my nephews Neri and Giovanni as his heirs. I received letters from Florence telling me that my name had been drawn as Vicegerent of the Upper Arno Valley, so I left Paris on the 12th of January and went to Avignon, and thence to Arles to call on King Louis, and then through Provence to Marseilles, where I planned to board one of the galleys that the King was having readied to send to Naples. I found that the galleys wouldn't be ready to set sail for a fortnight, and fearing to arrive too late to take up my office, which was supposed to begin on the first of March, I decided to go overland via Nice and the Italian Riviera. When I was two leagues from Nice, I sent ahead for a safe-conduct pass, but was refused. I went to a hill-town called Cagne, of which Giorgino and Onorato de' Grimaldi are the lords.[34] They were delighted to see me and welcomed me grandly. I asked them to help me fit out a vessel at Antibes so that I could bypass Nice and go straight to Monaco or Menton, and to get my horses through Nice by passing them off as their own. They said that they would be happy to do this. As we were deciding about this, a relative of theirs arrived from Nice; hearing our plan, he told us that there was a small galley anchored near Nice, for what purpose nobody knew. This aroused my suspicions, also because I heard that there were armed men all over the whole Riviera and that travelers were being robbed and murdered. I decided to return to Marseilles and wait for the galleys, which set sail on the 14th of February; I boarded a small vessel that was with them. We had so much bad weather that it took us 17 days before we reached Porto Pisano, and at one point it looked as if we were going to end up being blown all the way to the Barbary Coast. On account of the storm, the vessel in which I was traveling got separated from the three galleys during the night. Yet by the grace of God we reached Porto Pisano on the 2nd of March. On top of the great discomfort of being packed onto that vessel with the captain weeping

---

34. The Grimaldi had been made Florentine citizens around 1370. They were already lords, albeit contested, of Monaco and Menton.

and saying "We'll get blown to Barbary and be sold as slaves," you can imagine how I suffered and worried that our enemies would prevent my brothers from deferring the start of my term in office, so that I would arrive too late and be banned from holding office for two years.[35] I reached Pisa and heard from Filippo del Toccio that I had been granted an extension until the end of March. I came back to Florence, and was at my post on March 6, and, by the grace of God, I spent a very pleasant time there and did a good job, and returned thence with honor.

---

35. This was the punishment at the time for anyone who did not take up an office designated for him without making a formal refusal or resigning within the allotted time.

Donato Velluti

RICORDI

I.
Our Early History and Forefathers

December 1367

Man desires to know about his birth, his past, what his ancestors were like, and the wealth they acquired; and many times this avoids damage and prevents many errors. I, Donato, a judge, son of Lamberto di Filippo di Bonaccorso di Piero di Berto de' Velluti, finding myself to be the oldest member of our family, to perpetuate the memory of my descendants, and others of the Velluti family and everyone else, have decided to make a record of what I heard from my father and others older than myself, and of what I have read in letters, books, or other writings, as few as they may be, and what I have seen or learned myself; also because every man is mortal, and I am especially, as I suffer greatly with gout. I shall begin in the name of Our Lord Jesus Christ and his most holy and precious Mother, the Blessed Virgin Mary, his blessed apostles, and the precious confessor St. Nicholas and the precious virgin

St. Catherine and all the other saints in heaven, on the first of December, 1367.

I shall commence with our beginnings and early history and forefathers, writing of their goodness and their actions, mixing in with this their family relations. Then I shall say something about our property.

I found, from what I heard from my father and others older than I, who heard it from their elders — not in any documents — that our ancestors were originally from Simifonte di Valdelsa.[1] This was very rich land, and there were large, honorable families there, and many gentlemen with golden spurs. Simifonte had a big war with Florence; in the end Simifonte was razed to the ground by the Florentines, who decreed that it could never again be walled or built upon. The Florentine government kept the hill there from that time on, except for perhaps two or three years when the Florentine officials, who were deputed to be able to dispose of the property of the state, leased the hill and land to Filippo di Vanni da Petrognano. I know not whether our ancestors came thence to live in Florence before or after the place was destroyed. Whether we were originally from there or not, I do not give as certain, but only as hearsay. Not so long ago, some of our ancestors found people living there who bore our coat of arms; and for this reason it was believed that we and they had belonged to the same family.

What I found in authentic documents about my nearest ancestors (for I haven't found or heard anything about those who came before them) is that in a document made in 1244 or thereabouts, Donato, Bonaccorso, Cristiano, and Jacopo, the sons of Pero di Berto, entered into a certain agreement. I have found nothing from before the time of Berto, so I shall start from Donato, Bonaccorso, Cristiano, and Jacopo, from whom all of us in our family descended. They all lived together, and theirs was the tower that is in the street from the Canto de' Quattro Paoni (the second house on the right going toward the piazza where the Guicciardini

---

1. Dante, *Paradiso* XVI, 60-63, alludes to Lippo Velluti, one of Donato's ancestors from Simifonte or Semifonte in the Val d'Elsa.

live now). They did some trading and had several warehouses in Borgo San Jacopo. At that time there were no houses in the Via Maggio — just orchards — and it was called Casellina. But as time went on and their numbers and property increased, as I shall write at greater length, they began to build and live in the area where we live now. Since they began to build during the time of their children, first I shall write about their descendents and children. Since it appears that Jacopo died quite young, without marrying or having children, I shall not mention him at all, but shall begin with Donato, who, I find, was the eldest.

Donato had five sons: Mico, Ghino, Dietaiuti, Gherardino, and Lapo. Who his wife was, I can neither find nor ever heard; I think she was a sister or an aunt of Cino di Messire Dietisalvi Bonamichi.

I find that Bonaccorso, who was sometimes called Corso, from whom our side of the family descended, had only one son, who was sometimes called Lippo. I neither know nor can find who his wife was.

Cristiano had one son, who was named Velluto. I can neither find nor know who his wife was.

Some time passed, and Donato, Jacopo, Cristiano, and Ghino di Donato all died, and Velluto went off on his own, increasing his wealth and the size of his family. Bonaccorso's and Donato's children decided they wanted to have a better life, and to build their warehouses elsewhere. So they bought the land where the palazzo in the Via Maggio is today. This palazzo belongs to the sons of Piero and Matteo, and the land behind it, where my houses are, belonged to Lapo's sons. The land didn't cost much, because it was all orchards then; the area was called Casellina because of a little house that was nearby,[2] outside the city walls. The second circle of walls[3] behind which were the houses on this side of the Arno River — that is, the houses that used to belong to Cino Cerchi and today belong to Michele di Vanni di Messire Lotto

---

2. The word *casellina* means "little house."

3. These walls had one gate facing toward Pisa (from Borgo San Jacopo) and another toward Siena (from San Felice), between which the Velluti houses were located.

and the houses that used to belong to Lotto dell'Abraccia and today belong to the cloth cutter Francesco di Guidalotto, whom they call Rosso, on the back side. At that time, our ancestors were mocked, thus: "Look where the Velluti have gone to make their home!" For then it was held to be a beautiful, honorable palazzo, but in an out-of-the-way, almost rural location. When this palazzo and the houses behind it had been built, and Bonaccorso had gone to live there with his grandsons, and they brought their warehouses to that place, they created a new company, as I have mentioned earlier in this book. Little by little, this company began to trade in Bologna, Venice, Milan, Pisa, Genoa, Rome, Paris, France, and England. It was deemed unseemly that the letters that came from outside of Florence should be addressed to *Bonaccorso Velluti and Company, Casellina*; so, since the Via Maggio had been made wider and longer, and more houses had been built there, my great-grandfather Bonaccorso had his agents address letters to him thus: *Bonaccorso Velluti and Company, Via Maggiore*. That is how this street got its name, and it was called thus ever after; but because it later happened that with the passage of time, in spoken language all the names of people and things were shortened — Bonaccorso was called Corso, Filippo was called Lippo, Dietaiuti was called Duti, Gherardino was called Dino — the name of the street was shortened as well. Where it had been called Via Maggiore, it now came to be called Via Maggio.

II.
Madonna Diana and Her Turban

Madonna Diana, the sister of Donato and daughter of the late Mico, was the wife of Guerrucciolo de' Rossi. She had two sons, Tribaldo and Binguccio. Tribaldo's descendants today are Guerrieri and his children. Binguccio's descendants today are Amerigo, Bartolommeo, Pieraccino, and their children, as well as Madonna Filippa, the wife of Piero di Neri del Zanca. Their descendants were Binguccio, Pescaia, and Neri. Madonna Diana was a very good woman, and was very fond of me, for love of her brother; she kept me much with her at Boboli[4] when I was a boy. She always wore a massive turban on her head. On one occasion when she was at the old palazzo of the Rossi family across from the church of Santa Felicita, where the inn is today, a large stone fell from the top of the palazzo and hit her on the head. To Madonna Diana, it felt like dust that had been scratched up by chickens; so she said, "chick chick chick." It did her no other harm, on account of all the cloth she had on her head.

III.
Bonaccorso di Pietro: A Bold, Strong, Hearty Man

Bonaccorso di Pietro was a bold, strong, hearty man, and very able in the use of arms. He accomplished great feats of valor and gallantry, both in Florence and in other places. He had received so many wounds in battles and skirmishes that he had been stitched up all over his body. He was a great opponent of the Paterins[5] and heretics, when they were openly fighting about this type of thing in Florence, as I heard, at the time of St. Peter Martyr.[6]

Bonaccorso was tall in stature, with strong limbs, and well put together. He lived a full 120 years[7], but he was blind for the last 20 years of his life. He was called Corso; and I heard that when he was very old, he had become so stiff that he couldn't bend his body. He was also an experienced, honest merchant. He enjoyed such a good reputation that when a shipment of Milanese cloth arrived in Florence (for he ordered a great deal of cloth from Milan), he would sell out of it even before the bales were untied. He had

---

4. Where later the Pitti Palace and Boboli Gardens were built.
5. "Patarin" or "Paterin" was a term applied to Albigenses and other heretics.
6. A Dominican friar who was called to Florence by the Inquisition in 1243, and who promoted a citizens' crusade against the Paterins.
7. A typical exaggeration in this kind of family history.

a great deal of the cloth dyed here in Florence; and because he was so upright, I heard that a certain Giovanni del Volpe, who was a buyer of theirs, seeing him sell such a great quantity of this cloth, got the idea of making more profits for the company by having it dyed with weaker dyes at a lower cost. After some time had passed, the cloth didn't have the same durability as usual; seeking the reason why, they found that it was due to this Giovanni's slyness, and Corso wanted to kill him for it.

After he lost his eyesight, Bonaccorso stayed at home most of the time. He had the back part of the palazzo in the Via Maggio before it was divided up between him and his grandsons. There was a balcony along the length of the palazzo, which had three bedchambers on the back side. He would walk back and forth there every morning until he figured he had walked three or four miles. After his walk, he breakfasted, and his breakfast wasn't just two bread rolls. Then at midday he ate copiously, for he was a great eater. And thus he passed his days.

Now I want to tell you how he died. My father told me that one day Bonaccorso decided he wanted to go to the warming room;[8] while there, he struck his foot on something. When he returned and saw that on account of this injury he was unable to take his usual exercise, he immediately believed that he was going to die. It happened that at this time his son Filippo, who was my grandfather, was about to marry his second wife, Madonna Gemma de' Pulci. That day, Bonaccorso had jested a great deal, saying: "I, not my son, am the one who needs to take a wife," and many other witticisms. Lying on his bed, he decided to have himself carried to his lounging chair; so he called his grandsons — that is, my father and my uncle Gherardo — and leaning his hands and arms on their shoulders, suddenly the life went out of him on account of his great age, and he died; that was in 1296.

---

8. A *stufa secca*, a room warmed by hot air coming from below or the sides; see Bonaccorso Pitti, note 6, p. 90.

Donato Velluti

IV.
Donato's Brother Lottieri, the Augustinian Friar

After Friar Lottieri[9] returned from Paris,[10] he stayed in Florence most of the time. He was prior or provincial[11] several times, and very beloved and revered in the monastery, and was a great consolation to me and others. He was kind, friendly, and honest, without a bit of malice in him. He was stout, of average height, brawny, and full-figured. He had great illnesses, and several times we feared for his life. He was a great eater and drinker; indeed, he had an enormous appetite. He suffered from colic and gout. Finally, it pleased God to suddenly call my brother to him. On the 27th of March, 1367, Lottieri was in the second cloister, while the brothers were at vespers. He was at the foot of a pine tree in the cloister; there were no other friars around. He had a stick in his hand and was striking the tree to knock down the pine cones. He fell to the ground; when the friars returned from vespers, one of them saw him lying on the grass. Not recognizing Lottieri, the friar went up to him; realizing who it was, he immediately called the other friars. They carried him to his cell, where, on the doctor's advice, they rubbed him down and did the other necessary things. But in spite of everything they did, he never spoke or showed any sign of consciousness. According to what was said by Master Jacopo of Bologna, a most worthy physician, the infirmity that befell him is called apoplexy, which so alters a man that few survive it. He remained in that afflicted state until midnight, and then passed from this life; God keep his soul. This was a great blow and loss for me, and likewise for the monastery.[12] He was

---

9. Born in 1314, Lottieri entered the order of Augustinian friars at Santo Spirito in Florence around 1329-30.
10. Following the plague of 1348.
11. A monastic superior who has the direction of all the religious houses in a given province or district.
12. The monastery of Santo Spirito was hoping to make Lottieri a bishop. In 1351, the Florentine government recommended his promotion to bishop to the pope.

born on the feast of Our Lady[13] in August 1314, and passed from this life on the 27th of March 1367, at fifty-three years of age.

V.
Donato's Adventures as a Boy, and Later as a Young Judge at the Time of the Duke of Athens[14]

The time has now come for me to write about myself, Donato, a judge, the son of the late Lamberto Velluti, and about the descendants and relatives I acquired through my wife and children. It would be more seemly for someone else to write about me, rather than that I myself should do so; but my children are quite young, and know little about my affairs. So, since no one else knows my story, I have decided to write about a few things, politely passing over events that might lead too much to my praise or virtues. And if I should trespass in anything, I shall not do so to praise myself, but to record things that have occurred, since I believe that it will please my readers to know about them, and especially how and why they happened.

I was born on July 6, 1313, and was raised and educated mainly by my mother and my brother Filippo. I am of average height, with a fresh, rosy face, white complexion, and small limbs. When I was young and before I took a wife, I was very healthy, and didn't suffer any fever or other illness; I weighed very little, being quite thin. After I took a wife, for 7 or 8 years I suffered from stomach ailments and colic; then the humors that were creating these problems changed into gout, which has given me a great deal of discomfort; it began around 1347, when I was 34 or 35

---

13. The principal feast day of the Blessed Virgin Mary is August 15.

14. Gualtieri di Brienne (Walter of Brienne), who died in 1356. His father, with the aid of knights of the Fourth Crusade, had been lord of the so-called Duchy of Athens (in Byzantine territory), but was killed in battle and lost the duchy. Walter claimed the empty title.

years old, and causes me to have a little fever some times. God be praised, up to now He had spared me from illnesses with long-lasting fevers; in future, let Him do what He will.

It is true that when I was a boy of about ten or so, late one evening I was enticed by a citizen of Florence into going with him to carry some weapons outside the Ognissanti Gate along the banks of the Mugnone River. First he took me to the Carraia bridge; then, pretending to be afraid of the police, he took me all the way to the Ognissanti Gate, and thence along the Mugnone. Being foolish and eager to please, I let myself get caught in a trap. While we were going along the Mugnone toward Faenza, suddenly three men emerged from the fields. With knives drawn, they and the man who had enticed me there seized me, and kept me concealed in the Mugnone river-bed, for the city gate was closed. I was on foot, with a rope around my neck, all night long. Around dawn, we arrived near Pistoia. From thence we traveled until dinnertime to Borgo di Buggiano,[15] leading me to believe that we were in Peretola on the way to Florence; and they acted very kind and solicitous to me. Indeed, while we were staying at an inn, the innkeeper realized that I had been kidnapped and reported it to the *podestà*,[16] who immediately took me away from my captors and put me in the care of the leading farmer in the area, and put them in jail while he waited for a reply from Castruccio[17] about what he should do with me and the knaves who had kidnapped me, which I was not happy about. But when he was informed why I had been captured — that is, to demand ransom for my release — and how they would have mistreated me, taking me to Carafagnana, he was duly alarmed, and I was content. The answer came from Castruccio that the knaves should be released and that I should be taken to him at Lucca; the knaves also came to give their side of the story. Castruccio questioned me personally about how I had been captured and many other

---

15. In the province of Pistoia.
16. The chief magistrate elected annually in mediæval Italian towns and republics, with judicial functions and almost unlimited powers.
17. Castruccio Castracani, who ruled Lucca between 1308 and 1328.

things, and then sent me to stay with his wife and children. After I had been there for several days, he sent for me again and asked me if I wanted to stay with him. I said that I would be happy to do as he pleased and to follow his orders, but I begged His Lordship to let me return to Florence to console my mother and brothers. He agreed, and immediately called for two horses and a servant to take me back to Florence. We wanted to give the servant some cloth to make clothes for himself, but he wouldn't take it, because Castruccio had told him not to accept any gifts. My brother Filippo accompanied Castruccio's servant back as far as Santa Gonda, and wanted to give him 25 florins, but he wouldn't take them. My friends and relatives were overjoyed at my return, and Castruccio was greatly praised and esteemed by everyone. We had the knaves banished from Florence.

After my return, I began to study grammar and then logic. I lived in Bologna for eight or nine years, and had many discomforts there. I stayed on at the University of Bologna, except that one year I returned to Florence on account of the unrest when the Cardinal of Ostia, who was lord of Bologna and the Romagna, was expelled by the Church and the Cardinal Legate. I stayed in Florence for about six months, and then returned to Bologna, where I remained until May 1339. Then I left, because Bologna and the University had been placed under interdict. I went to Careggi, outside the city walls of Florence, to the home of Gherardo Manetti, where with Ugo di Piero, the son of Messire Oddo Altoviti, I studied the book that we had been reading that year in Bologna, which is called "The Old Digest." If it hadn't been for the fact that I couldn't continue studying in Bologna — for it was my last year of study —, I would have taken my doctorate in a public ceremony, although I had already paid the fee of 40 florins, which my father had sent me, to take the private examination. But seeing that most of the students had already departed, and since the public examination for the doctorate is a mere formality, I didn't take it.

We stayed at Careggi until October, when we left. Since the University of Bologna had not been reinstated, Messire Ugo went to Pisa to finish his studies, because a great legal scholar, Rinieri da Forlì,[18] was there, with many students. I returned in secret to Florence, and stayed locked up in the house unbeknownst to anyone. I studied all winter and emerged publicly in the summer.

It happened that Piero Velluti[19] was going to take up the duties of captain of the guard at Colle[20] in November; at the last minute the judge who was supposed to go with him backed out, and Piero couldn't find another judge. So he hounded my father until he told him where I was. Piero came to speak to me and asked me to serve for two weeks or a month, until he could find another judge. I went, and I liked my chambers, and the office wasn't so onerous that I couldn't continue to study; so I decided to stay there for the whole duration of the office. In the meantime, I studied law with several knowledgeable local notaries. After the office terminated, on the calends of May we returned to Florence; thanks be to God, I entered the city late in the evening. I remained in the house, without going out, until the feast of the Ascension,[21] in May of 1339, with no pomp. The next day I went to the Public Palace, where I was seen and honored by judges and notaries alike; and practicing the law between the Public Palace and the Signory, I was in great demand. My father wanted to give me a wife; but I, wishing to honor my brothers, who were older than I and were not in Florence at the time, did not obey him. I still regret this, for though he was very happy with me, I wish I could have given him that consolation while he was alive. The plague of 1340 arrived, and he passed from this life and I was left alone in the house, with no woman to help me. The following November, Piccio[22] returned, and I wanted him to take a wife; but since he hadn't yet made a start in a profession, he did not wish to take one. So I, encouraged by friends and relatives, made up my mind to take a wife, and the following January I took as my lady and wife Madonna Bice, the daughter of the late Messire

---

18. The famous jurist Ranieri degli Arsendi da Forlì.
19. Pietro di Gherardino di Donato, a second cousin of the writer's father.
20. Colle di Val d'Elsa, a town in the province of Siena.
21. May 24.
22. One of Velluti's brothers.

Covone de' Covini — a dear, wise, very good woman, though not a beautiful one. I was very happy with her, and while she lived every good befell me, both in terms of my family and my advancement in the world.

On the feast of All Saints in November of that year, the Bardi and the Frescobaldi were driven out by the fury of the populace, because those families wished to overturn the popular government. For this reason, a body of 40 good men was created, and they were given a great deal of power. I was one of this group, and succeeded to many other public offices, such as the Council of Twelve of Pistoia and Arezzo, and many others.[23] I was honored more than was seemly, considering my youth and lack of sense.

After the affair of the purchase of Lucca by Messire Mastino, and the subsequent war with Pisa, and our defeat by Lucca and loss of that city, Florence was in a bad state. On the feast day of Our Lady in September, the Duke of Athens was made lord, or rather tyrant, of Florence. He made me one of the first priors, although I was very worried about it; when he sent for me, I was very afraid. I got very much into his good graces, both because he found me to be honest and loyal and because once peace had been made with Pisa, Duke Guarnieri[24] formed a large company of soldiers from the men who had been discharged after that war. In order to prevent Guarnieri from doing damage in the countryside, the Duke gave him money, though he himself was quite short of funds. Since I had about 400 florins, without him asking me I offered them to him, and he accepted them and then immediately had them returned to me without asking for them again. For this reason and others, he made me Advocate of the Poor;[25] and when my office as prior ended, he ordered all of his doorkeepers and servants to give me access to his private

---

23. Velluti was prior from October 14 to December 14, 1341; he was elected podestà with two other lawyers against Gherardo Vecchio on December 29, 1941; he went as ambassador to Prato on February 4, 1342; he went with other Florentines to elect the new *podestà* on March 6, 1342; and was one of the Twelve Good Men appointed in April 1342 to oversee Pistoia for 3 months.

24. Werner or Warner, Duke of Urslingen, a German soldier of fortune.

apartments. When people saw how much I was in favor, I became in great demand; if I had been interested in money, I could have gained a great deal. But I did a lot of favors for many people, and bestowed many honors on the citizens of Florence, always remembering the common people as well. The Duke's advisers were greatly displeased at this, for they wanted neither equals nor colleagues. It was on account of their bad counsel that the Duke ended badly, for they advised him to be a tyrant rather than a ruler, and to make himself rich rather than to govern, and they led him to do evil deeds. Seeing this, and realizing that he was becoming very unpopular with the citizens of Florence, I slowly began to distance myself from him, but not totally. I asked him for nothing, I never went to the Public Palace except to hear Mass[26] on feast days, and on rare occasions for festivities, when I would pay my respects to him and then leave. Continuing his evil operations, the Duke was driven from power; the uprising began on the feast day of St. Anne[27] in July 1343. After he was expelled, the office of the Fourteen was created, and they were given full powers.

---

25. This seems to have been an institution created by the Duke of Athens in an attempt to curry favor with the under classes.
26. Evidently in the chapel of the Signori in the Palazzo Vecchio.
27. July 26.

Goro Dati

SECRET BOOK

I.
Company Troubles, Especially in Spain

Making a rough estimate of my assets, I find that when Michele left the company on the 1st of January, 1392, and I remained, I was left with a net amount of around 800 florins that would have been mine if I had left the company. In fact, I had made no profit, but rather would have had to make good part of the debts amounting to about 950 florins that were owed to the company in Catalonia and elsewhere, which were not recoverable at that time. We discovered this later when on account of Antonio di Segna's treachery we decided we should check what we really had in cash assets in the company. This was why I resolved to endure everything for these last 2 years, and to stay with the company and put up with Antonio di Segna and everything else, for I felt myself to be too short of money to be able to do things my own way should there have been a need of it. And I've been hoping that Matteo would help me, and that I would be able to send Simone to Valencia so that he can help me with my affairs here. I pray God to grant that it should be so.

After that, in 1393 I received my wife's[1] dowry, which was 800 florins, and had profits of 162 florins, and this year I made 325 florins in profits, which comes to 1,287 florins. On the other hand, I made two payments totaling 1,425 florins as appears under Expenditures on folio 3. This includes my losses when 250 florins were stolen from me on the Riviera, and the purchase of the farm for 275 florins, and the 100 florins I lent to Michele's heir. Thus while in 1392 I was owed 950 florins and owed about 150 florins, since then I find my debits exceeding my credits by about 140, for a total debit of 390 florins. I estimate that in the last eight months that I have been in business on my own, I have made good my losses and wiped out the debt, or at least I will have when the ventures I have embarked upon have been concluded. So I have preserved my capital. Would to God and the Virgin Mary that I were certain of retaining my capital in cash on the Wrst of January 1395 — that is, that my debits would not exceed my credits since the time I went into partnership with Michele. But God will grant us His grace as He has always done. I am not counting the 950 florins and 25 *soldi* owed to me by debtors, which I mention on folio 6, because I cannot use them.

After that year, by the grace of God I did better than I had anticipated, because the business in Valencia turned out well for me. And I find that I have been able to transfer 200 florins from the credit side and deduct them from the debits, as appears under Expenditures on folio 3.

The new company is recorded on folio 6.

---

1. Dati's second wife, Betta di Mario di Lorenzo Villanuzzi.

Goro Dati

II.
Confessions and Resolutions

January 1, 1404.

Because in this wretched life our sinfulness subjects us to many tribulations of the soul and passions of the body, if it weren't for the grace of God, who deigns to assist our weakness with his mercy by revealing to our mind what we should do and by sustaining us, we would perish daily. I realize that I have already passed the age of 40 with little obedience to God's commandments; not trusting in my own powers of getting on the right path, but hoping to advance by degrees along that path, I resolve from this day to refrain forever from going to the shop on solemn feast days declared by the holy Church. Nor will I conduct any business, nor allow others to work for me for temporal gain, with this exception: in cases of extreme necessity, each time I transgress I shall distribute alms of one gold florin to God's poor on the following day. I have written this down so that I may keep this resolution in mind, and to shame myself if I should break it.

Also, in memory of the Passion of Our Lord Jesus Christ by whose merits we are freed and saved, that He may forever save us from every evil passion by His mercy and grace, from this day I resolve in my heart to keep Friday as a day of chastity in perpetuity — by Friday I also mean Friday night — and to abstain from any act of carnal pleasure. May our Lord grant me the grace to do so; and if it should happen that I should fall, either through inattention or forgetfulness, the next day I engage to give twenty *soldi* to God's poor for each time, and to say the Our Father and the Hail Mary 20 times.

I also resolve this day to do a third thing while I am healthy and able to, remembering that we need Almighty God to take care of us every day. Each day I wish to honor God by giving some alms or saying some prayers, or some other pious action. And if by inadvertence I should fail to do so, as soon as I realize it, that same day or the next I must give alms of at least five *soldi* to God's poor.

These, however, are not vows;[2] but I am doing this to help myself keep these good intentions to the best of my ability.

May 3rd of the year of our Lord 1412.

On April 28 my name was drawn as Standard-bearer of my Company.[3] Until that time, I had not been sure whether my name had been put forward and yet I desired it both for my own honor and that of those who shall remain after me. I remember that Stagio, my father, held many offices in his lifetime, and was several times a consul of the Guild of Porta Santa Maria, and of the Merchants' Council of Five, and a tax official and a chamberlain; but he was never drawn for any of the Colleges in his life, though shortly after his death he was drawn as a prior. And I remember that eight years ago I underwent many adversities on account of my business in Catalonia, and that last year I had to take care not to be arrested for debt to the Commune of Florence. On the very day that I was chosen for this office, a quarter of an hour before, I had finished paying my debt to the City thanks to a reprieve, which was an inspiration from God, may He always be praised and blessed. Now that I can secure other offices, it seems to me that I have received a great blessing, and I should be content with being able to say that I have sat once in the Colleges and should aspire no further. So, lest I be ungrateful or become too hungry for power (for the more men have, the more they want), I have decided and resolved that henceforth I shall never ask anyone to help me obtain whatever public offices there might be up for selection or voting, but rather I shall let those who are in charge of

---

2. That is, solemn promises to God, the breaking of which implies a mortal sin.

3. In the constitution of 1250, the people of Florence were divided up into twenty "companies;" these were reduced to 19 in 1306. Dati's *gonfalone* or district was Ferze, in the Santo Spirito quarter.

such things do their job, and abide by God's will. I shall accept whatever public or guild office for which I might be chosen, not refusing the work but obeying the call, and I shall do whatever good I can. In this way I shall avoid the vice of ambition and presumptuousness, and shall live in freedom without having to demean myself by begging for favors. And if I should depart from this resolve, each time I do, I condemn myself to give two gold florins in alms within a month. I have made this resolution in my fiftieth year.

This same day, for the good and security of my conscience, knowing myself to be weak in the face of sin, I resolve never to accept any office, should my name be drawn, in which I would have the power to exercise the death penalty. And if I should depart from this resolution, I condemn myself to give twenty-five gold florins to the poor within three months of accepting such an office. And I shall in no wise attempt to influence those who make the selections for such offices, either by asking them to put or not to put in my name, but shall let them do as they see fit. And every time I might fail to do so, I condemn myself to give a gold florin to the poor.

III.
The Company in Danger of Failing

Company with Piero Lana. 1408.

The accounts for the shop and for the last company are written above, on folio 8.

Because things went badly for us in Barcelona, and on account of the lawsuit here that followed, and the suspicions about what Simone was doing, and the evil rumors that many people were spreading, we couldn't get any credit. So we were forced to withdraw from business in order to pay all our creditors, and we got money from friends and by using every ploy we could, suffering losses, interest, and expense in order to avoid bankruptcy and shame. And although my partner[4] would have preferred to go bankrupt in order to avoid some losses and expenditure, I decided that I would rather lose all my money than lose my honor. With great effort, I held on until we paid everyone off, and I had only my partners left to deal with. May the Lord be praised and blessed for it.

I truly believe that if I had been able to send Simone the silk and gold cloth that he was supposed to sell to the King, he would have succeeded in bringing his business to a successful conclusion. But I was unable to do so — indeed, I had to refrain from business activity until the year 1405 — for the disputes and lawsuits began, and I had to sell what I had here in order to pay my debts. Thus I could not send him the things he was expecting from me, which he had promised to the King, and his business began to fall apart and to encounter great difficulties, so there was never any way to make it right again, and things went from bad to worse.

Since Simone's affairs were going badly, he could not fill our orders and remittances, and my partner became impatient and began to complain loudly and to behave in a way that was contrary to our business interests. Proceedings were taken against him by Antonio di Messire Bartolomeo and two other powerful companies for an earlier transaction they had had with me, and there was a dispute and lawsuit about that transaction. I had gone to Spain; Piero defended our interest badly, did not produce our accounts as evidence, and merely tried to show that he was not liable. The judgment went against him, and he had to pay up. Of the 500 florins we owed, I had already paid back 300 florins to their agents in Spain, so we only owed them 200 florins more; but they were awarded two thousand two hundred florins. I do not think that such a thing was ever heard of, and I hope it may bring them bad luck. Yet we are the ones who suffer from it, and the fault lies with my partner and his contrary ways.

---

4. Piero Lana.

I decided to go to Spain to see if there was some way to prevent us losing everything there; and I left Florence with Pagolo Mei[5] on the 12th of November 1408. Pagolo had decided to go sometime before, and when he told me this, I decided to go as well. We traveled by land, and had a very wearisome journey in harsh winter weather, arriving in Murcia on December 30th. We found Simone there, and we all had high hopes for his business. But it didn't turn out well for us, on account of the falsity of the Spaniards; it certainly was through no fault of his, but because he was treated unfairly. I was back safe and sound in Florence by March 15, 1410, but all I had acquired on my trip was toil and sorrow.

It then transpired that my partner Piero Lana kept pursuing me in every way he could, and he accused me before the Merchant's Court as a bankrupt and had me publicly denounced by their herald. But he didn't succeed in getting a judgment against me, which would have been a great iniquity, for I had not gone bankrupt but had returned from abroad to settle my accounts with him and to do whatever I could to remedy things. He died of the plague in July 1411, while the lawsuit was going on.

Later I came to an agreement with Piero's brother Papi, in his name and the name of Piero's children. I have recorded this on folio 15 of my long account book.

---

5. A friend and business associate whom Dati mentions several times.

Francesco Datini

Last Will and Testament

Foundation of the Hospice for the Poor[1]

The Testator, Francesco, for the love of God and so that God's poor would be given what he himself had received as a gift and blessing from God, wished and ordered that his chief residence in Prato, with its garden and the house opposite, loggias, rooms, and furnishings, should always belong to the poor as a private hospice, granary, and home, in no way subject to the Church or to ecclesiastical authority or Church prelates or other people of the Church; and that it should in no wise ever become the property of the Church, but that it should always belong to the poor, for the perpetual use of the poor of Jesus Christ, for their everlasting nourishment and emolument. Francesco left, destined, and ordered that his home be used in every best way and for every best reason; with the ways, order, agreements, and conditions in the present testament set forth below. To distinguish this house from the other hospices for the poor in the city of Prato, it shall be called *The Hospice of the Poor of Francesco di Marco*.

For this House, Granary, or Hospice of the Poor, Francesco

---

1. This is the second part of the last will and testament of Francesco di Marco Datini, dictated by him on July 31, 1410 to Lapo Mazzei, his notary, friend, and assiduous correspondent. The official text was in Latin, but Lapo attached this version in Italian, which probably retains dispositions dictated to him orally by Francesco.

ordered that land and buildings be purchased with any monies that derive from the estate of the said Francesco by the undersigned Executors or Governors of the House, who shall be listed below. The said testator Francesco gave, consigned, left, and adapted for the love of God, to the said House or Hospice, which is his sole beneficiary, all of his property and buildings wherever they may be, both present and future. He forbade the sale, cession, or long-term lease of the said real property, so that their fruits might feed God's poor in perpetuity. And if, contrary to said prohibition, any of his property should be given away or leased, then he ordered that said property should be given to the Guild of Orsanmichele. It was his wish that said property and lands and whatever they produced should be given to, spent for, and distributed to the poor of Jesus Christ, both the poor who are publicly known and those who keep their poverty secret out of shame, as is done at the other Hospice of the poor in Prato. This shall be executed by four of the best and most honest citizens of Prato, who should be elected or named in the general council of that city every year, as shall be related below. Each year the city council of Prato shall select the appropriate directors of the foundation, and determine their removal. Francesco decreed that this election should be done with the full mandate and authority, and in accordance with the wishes of the said city of Prato; always excepting the things that are contained in the present last will and testament.

Since he has great confidence in the city of Prato and its leaders, Francesco left the maintenance, protection, governance, and rule of the Hospice to the said city, at the expense of the foundation. He put the rule, governance, and administration of the Hospice entirely and in perpetuity in the hands of the city of Prato, including the collection of his debts and accounts, just as he would have done during his life. This he did so that, for the love that he bears the city of Prato and her citizens, the proper things should be done for the Hospice, and so that what has been set forth above and below might be carried out. With the assistance of the city of Prato, the Hospice should be protected from any power or magnate that might wish to take it over under a secular or ecclesiastical veil. Francesco entreated and admonished the city of Prato to protect his sole heir, the Hospice, from any damages resulting from payments or promises made by him, the Testator; and that the sums paid and received and the amounts promised should be duly settled within the proper amount of time.

The Testator wished and declared that at the time of the annual appointment of the four elders who are to administer the foundation to the best of their abilities and according to the dictates of their conscience, in the general council of the city of Prato, the following persons should be present in order to vote or to speak during the deliberations: Chiarito di Matteo Chiariti, Lionardo di Ser Tommaso di Giunta, Barzalone di Spedalieri, Ser Amelio di Messire Lapo, Messire Piero Rinaldeschi, Giovanni di Bartolomeo, Stefano di Ser Piero, Messire Torrello di Messire Niccolò, Messire Bonaccorso di Messire Niccolò, Martino di Niccolò Martini, Bartolomeo di Matteo Convenevoli, and Biagio di Bartolo, all from Prato; in their absence, their descendants on the male side should attend, but not more than one per family, and they must be of legal age. Francesco named the aforementioned men and their descendents as continual protectors, watchful guardians, and loving defenders of the Hospice and of his last wishes. Nothing should be done outside of the general council of the city of Prato or against the wishes of the four directors. Nevertheless, when their term of office comes to an end, the aforementioned four directors must render to the city of Prato an accounting of what they have done.

As a precaution, and to expedite assistance to the poor of the Hospice as well as the management thereof as mentioned above, Francesco ordered that whoever should become the four directors of the foundation after his death should review and calculate and settle all of his accounts and collect from the city of Florence and its administrators the payments, gifts, and interest on Francesco's credits in any of the public funds of Florence, present and future; even those monies that are held as taxes or duties, and negotiable titles.[2] They should properly settle these and any other

---

2. *Accattoni* were negotiable titles for the reimbursement of forced loans; the *Monte dei Prestanzoni* was a public debt that returned 6%.

debts or obligations so that Francesco's name is no longer associated with them and so that no one else is affected by the aforementioned loans. He prays the four directors of the foundation to act benevolently toward his poor friends, who are well known to Madonna Margherita, Luca, Barzalone, and Lionardo.[3]

So that the doors of the Hospice might always be open to receive people coming and going, and to keep an eye and ear on things useful to the foundation, he stipulated that the City of Prato should find a guardian, be it a married man or single, of good status and reputation, whose sole care should be the Hospice. This guardian should be given a residence somewhere in the Hospice, and some kind of stipend for his living expenses; the amount and schedule of payments shall be determined by the city of Prato.

Francesco ordered that the aforementioned Madonna Margherita, along with Luca, Barzalone, and Lionardo, and those who should survive them, be the executors and agents of the aforementioned things, that debtors pay and that goods be purchased with the monies that shall be derived from the said payments, gifts, interest, and credits, and that his last will and testament as herein written be executed in its entirety; for these four persons are fully informed of Francesco's wishes in almost everything. He requests that the city of Prato confer with them and with those who survive them about any of the things to be done in his name that may be of particular weight or importance. And he wishes that, if those things should not be done, the four aforementioned persons should be able to lodge a complaint, wherever necessary, and, should they deem it essential, even to execute the present last will and testament themselves. This in the event that the will should not be duly executed and that the things that Francesco ordered should not be done with the diligence and in the way and form ordered by him. In such a case, these four persons and their survivors may collect debts, finish making payments to the

---

3. Francesco's four executors were his wife, Madonna Margherita; his partner, Luca del Sera; his son-in-law, Lionardo di Ser Tommaso di Giunta; and his partner and steward in Prato, Barzalone di Spedalieri.

Francesco Datini

Public Fund, handle Francesco's credits, loans, negotiable titles, monies, and capital, and even finish making payments said to be sustained by another instrument. They should do all of the things that the testator, had he lived, would do; and to pay off Francesco's loans with the money as long as it lasts, or to put it at the disposition of the Hospice in order to execute his will. In such cases, these four persons and their survivors will act as executors after the death of the trustor, make the said payments to the Public Fund, and do the other things that are granted to the city of Prato or to the four to be selected by the said city, to do. They can also name another executor as they see fit, and they can remove the substitutes and appoint others.

For all his other goods and property, accounts, and holdings present and future, for the love of God Francesco named the said Hospice as his sole heir, which as above is designated in perpetuity, for the future use and needs of the poor of Jesus Christ, and the said poor as ordered above in the section that begins "And the said testator Francesco," etc. Francesco declared that it was his wish and intention that the Hospice be completely private and not sacred, and that in no way and for no reason should it be called ecclesiastical, but rather designated as secular, for the love of God, for the aforementioned use in perpetuity; nor should it be subject in any way to the Church or the clergy. Francesco desired that his last will and testament be kept on public view at the Hospice, in book form, attached by a chain, so that his wishes would be known to everyone, and that it should not be easily removable from thence. He also desired that every year the names of the aforementioned four appointed directors should be written in this book, as well as other things of which it shall please the city of Prato to keep a record in the future.

Finally, as on another occasion he said he had taken counsel about this, the aforementioned testator entreats the councilors, the city of Prato, and the four men who shall be elected directors of the foundation, and all his other aforementioned executors, to be very careful not to raise any altar in the Hospice, nor to turn it into an oratory or any type of ecclesiastical place, or do anything else by which the Hospice might be construed as an ecclesiastical place. Nor should any evil people, under the title of benefice, enter or occupy the said Hospice, which is entirely contrary to the testator's wishes. If any impediment to this should arise (may it please God to do away with it), Francesco's desire was that every effort and expenditure be made from his estate to prevent this from occurring.

This is the last will and testament of Francesco di Marco Datini.

Lapo di Giovanni Niccolini de' Sirigatti
Book of Family Affairs

I.
Ruzza's Revenge

Here I shall write about our ancestors, the ones I know about from the beginning of our family history all the way down to myself, Lapo. And I shall begin with the man who was the founder of our side of the family: Ruzza d'Arrigo di Luchese di Bonavia de' Sirigatti.[1] Ruzza had two brothers, one of whom was the prior of San Pietro a Scheraggio and rector of Antella. His name was Messire Bonavia, and the other brother's name was Luchese. When their father Arrigo died, they divided up his estate. The prior gave his portion to Luchese, either because he liked him better, or because Luchese had a greater need of it, for he had no fewer than seven sons and many daughters. At that time, the Guelphs were exiled for the first time,[2] and the prior was sent away from his church by the Cavigniano family. Later, when the Guelphs returned, the

---
1. According to Passerini, Ruzza lived between 1253 and 1293; Gamurrini thinks he lived a little earlier.
2. Probably after the defeat of the Florentine Guelphs near Siena at Montaperti, "the hill of death," on September 4, 1260.

Siminetti family and our own ancestors restored him to his church, where he stayed until the end of his life. Luchese and his sons had many descendants, many of whom are still here today; but since they don't have anything to do with our affairs, I shall skip over them and return to Ruzza, the founder of my side of the family. He was a big man, handsome and strong, and lived about a hundred and thirty years.[3] I know this from Giovanni my father, who saw him when he was completely bedridden. Ruzza had a son named Niccolino, whom he married to a daughter of the Scolari family in order to make peace with that family.

The reason is this: It seems that one of the Scolari family was out hunting, and so was one of Ruzza's nephews. A dispute arose about some prey, for both had let their dogs loose, and they had come from opposite sides. The argument grew heated; the man from the Scolari family, who was carrying a spear, struck the other man with it and killed him. Then to mock them he sent to Ruzza's family to ask for the spear back, for he had left it in the body of the dead man, for which Ruzza did not rest until he and his men killed the man who had killed his nephew, at the foot of Passigniano in a stream called the Rimaggio. Then he sent a message of his own to the Scolari, telling them to go to the Rimaggio and they would find their spear, for Razza killed the man with the same spear with which he had killed his nephew. The Scolari were outraged, for they were a powerful family at that time, and if the Buondelmonti family hadn't come to our family's aid, they would have been undone. But they made peace between the two families, and Ruzza married his young son Niccolino to the sister of the Scolari who had been killed, and peace was made between them . . .

---

3. This kind of exaggeration is not unusual.

Lapo Niccolini de' Sirigatti

II.
Property Transactions

In 1417 Monna Antonia, the daughter of the late Ser Giovanni di Ser Piero Gucci de' Sirigatti and of Monna Ghita, took over the estate of Ser Francesco, her brother, who had died intestate. Monna Antonia then took action against me about a house that I had bought from Ser Francesco; the purchase of this house is recorded on folio 47 of this book. Monna Antonia was very wrong to sue me for this house, to the detriment of her soul; because after he sold it to me, Ser Francesco returned the money that I had given him as part of the payment for the house, as we had agreed between us, and I insisted that I wanted to return the deeds of the house to him. Ser Francesco replied: "Lapo, you can see that there is going to be a plague in this year 1417. If I die, I trust you and want you to give this house, which my father built, to Francesco di Ser Niccolò di Ser Piero Gucci Sirigatti, my cousin; and have papers drawn up for this. And if Francesco should die without any legitimate male heirs, I want the house to go to you and to your children and heirs. So I in no wise want the deeds back, because I trust you." And he was right to trust me, for I would have followed all his instructions to the letter. Monna Antonia petitioned me four times, and I was forced to come to an agreement with her. This was during the time that Niccolò da Uzzano was chief magistrate in Florence.

III.
Lapo's Son, a Great Waster of
His Own and Others' Money

Almighty God called my son Niccolaio to him on Saint Lucy's day, 13 December 1417. May God grant great pardon to his soul, with His blessing and mine. Niccolaio was born on 29 March

1386, as appears on folio 19 of this book. He lived in this world for 31 years, 8 months, and 14 days. He had neither wife nor children, nor did he make a will, although I had made him independent, for he had nothing of his own and he had dissipated and squandered more of my money than was his fair share. And I have written in some of my books part of what he squandered, for although he was a man of understanding, and very talented, he was a great waster of his own and others' money. For he cared little for anything except following his own appetites and desires, and gave me a great deal of trouble while he lived in this miserable world.

Bernardo Machiavelli

RICORDI

I.
An Affair with a Servant Girl

I record on this 17th day of November 1475 that on Wednesday the 25th of last month, when I returned in the morning from Santo Andrea,[1] my wife[2] told me that because of certain signs that she had seen, she thought that Lorenza, a servant in our house whom we call Nencia di Lazerino, had acted dishonorably, for she believed her to be pregnant. My wife described the signs to me, and I told her to question the girl, and in one way or another, by threats or blandishments, to find out the truth. I went out, and when I returned at about the hour of vespers, she told me that she had called the girl into her room and between soft words and threats she had got it out of her that it was true that she was big with child, and that the father was Niccolò d'Alessandro

---

1. Sant'Andrea in Percussina, seven miles from Florence (near San Casciano), where the Machiavelli family owned land and where Niccolò retreated for long periods of time, writing extensively.
2. Bartolomea Nelli, who wrote prose and poetry. She would die in 1496, four years before her husband.

Machiavelli.[3] When my wife asked her how the thing had come about, the girl told her that after we returned from the country last year on the 8th of November, she had gone out at night many times through the window onto the roof or through the little window near the fireplace in the kitchen to Niccolò's house to be with him, especially during the time that my wife had been big with child, and after she gave birth; and that last May and June, when Niccolò's wife had been ill, Niccolò had come in many times through the little window and had his way with her on the hearth in the kitchen.

When I heard this, I went out to find Giovanni Nelli, my wife's brother, and it so happened that his brother Carlo was in Florence, having come to visit from Pisa. I told them the story and asked them to come the next day to dine with me to discuss the matter and to take whatever action they thought best. I did this because Giovanni had found the girl and had asked her father, who was a friend of his, to send her to me. The next day they came and dined with me; after we had eaten, I called Nencia into my room with the two of them and my wife and questioned her. She made the same reply as she had to my wife, and although Giovanni and Carlo and I warned her many times to watch what she said and that it didn't seem likely to us that Niccolò, who had a young, pretty wife, would have gone after her, she made the same reply. She also said that when Niccolò's household was in the country (for most of the time they stay at Colombaia)[4] he would climb up on the balcony and call to her through the iron bars of the window in her bedchamber, and they were together 2 or 3 times every week, and that the truth was that she was pregnant by Niccolò and that he had promised to give her a cloak and a wool dress. I sent Nencia out of the room and Giovanni and Carlo told me that I should go to Niccolò and tell him the state of affairs and what the girl was saying, and then I should tell them what he said, after which Giovanni wanted to talk to him

---

3. A cousin of Bernardo (Bernardo's grandfather and Niccolò's great-grandfather were brothers), then twenty-six years old.

4. Not far from Sant'Andrea in Percussina.

himself. I agreed, but told them that I absolutely did not want the girl in my house any longer, and that we should inform her mother, who is a member of Giovanni's household, and also her father, and they should come for her. They replied that I should talk to Niccolò first and then we would do whatever was necessary.

So, on Saturday the 28th, the evening of St. Simon's day, around 4 in the afternoon, I went out; as I was walking toward the Ponte Vecchio I ran into Niccolò coming toward me in the square of Santa Felicita. I told him that I wanted to speak to him about Nencia and what she had said. He replied that he had wanted to tell me about this for more than six months and he himself didn't know why he hadn't done so. But the reason was that more than six months earlier, Francesco Renzi, whom they call Agata, a nephew of the doctor Maestro Raffaello da Terranuova, had asked Niccolò to leave him alone with Nencia in in his house in Florence when his family was in the country (and he often left him alone there, for they were fast friends) and that Nencia would go out over the roof of our house into Niccolò's house to be with Francesco. This had happened many times since I had returned from the country, and the truth was, Niccolò said, that he had never had anything to do with the girl, but that Francesco had, and that his only fault in the business was not having told me about it. I was very upset, and told him that he had done me a great injury, great in any case but more so in a next-door neighbor and a close relative, and that I had never done such a thing to him or to his father, and I didn't understand how he could have so little regard for me. For if it were true that it had been Francesco, who was often with me both here in Florence and in the country, he had never given me to understand it, so that I could take measures so that my house wouldn't be used as a bordello. I told him that he should think hard about this affair, for this girl wasn't from the Mugello[5] but from Pistoia, of good people but poor; that her father and brothers might want to avenge her; that I absolutely didn't want her in my house any longer; and that the

---

5. According to at least one scholar, in Bernardo's day this was a place known for women of easy virtue.

best thing for me to do was to tell Giovanni Nelli, who had gotten her for me, or to have her father and mother come and take her away. I said that I didn't know what the father would do when he heard the girl's story, for she said that Niccolò was the father; and that he should think it over. Niccolò replied that he realized he had done me an injury, but that the truth was that it had been Francesco who had sinned with her, and that he, Niccolò, had only erred in not telling me about it, and that it wasn't his responsibility, for he had a wife and sisters. He said he would think about it and would see me again. The 24th hour had already rung, and he didn't want to stay inside the city,[6] so he left, returning to Colombaia, where he said his family was staying.

On Monday the 30th of October I went to Giovanni Nelli and told him that I had spoken to Niccolò and related everything he had answered to me. Giovanni said I should be patient, that he wanted to speak to Niccolò himself. On the morning of the 31st, walking toward the Ponte Vecchio I met Niccolò outside the palazzo of Mariotto de' Rossi. He said to me: "I hadn't seen you again, but now I want to tell you why I never told you about Nencia and Agata. As you know, Francesco Agata lives in the same house with Doctor Raffaello; please don't say anything about what I'm going to tell you to the doctor. Francesco had a pretty girl in his household whom I wanted for my own pleasure, and Francesco acted as middleman for me. So, since he had done me that favor, I went along with what he was doing with Nencia." He said that later the thing had come out and that there had been the devil of a fuss, but that he had extricated himself. "So," he told me, "you see the reason for the injury I did you, which I know is a great one." I replied that this was a nice alibi, and that the girl was telling a different story, that he himself was the father; and that if things were really as he said they were, I was even more offended, for he had dared to act as pimp for Agata with my maidservants and to turn my house into a bordello with people coming and going at all hours of the night. I told him that I had told Giovanni Nelli about the affair, and that I wanted Giovanni

---

6. The city gates of Florence were locked each evening.

to send for the girl's father and give her back to him, for I didn't want her any more; and that Giovanni had told me he wanted to speak to Niccolò before he told the girl's father, to see if a scandal could be avoided. And I added that he should think it over and take care to find some kind of a solution with Giovanni, for I didn't want the girl in my house for anything. Having said this, I left him.

Then on Friday the 3rd of the present month Giovanni came to supper and to spend the night at my home, and told me that that evening he had been in the New Market with Niccolò Machiavelli, and that Niccolò had told him the same story he had told me on the 29th and 31st of last month; and moreover, that he had said to Niccolò that he thought in order to avoid a big scandal, which might come out if the girl's father found out, they should find a woman whom she could stay with until she gave birth and see to it that the girl had 25 florins to marry on right after the baby was born, in order to save Giovanni's honor, for he was the one who had given the girl to me. Niccolò said he liked the idea; still insisting that he hadn't been the one to get the girl pregnant, but that it had been Francesco Agata, he said that he wanted to talk to Francesco and see if he could convince him to do what Giovanni said, and that he would let Giovanni know in a few days; so that's how they left things.

Then on Monday, the 6th of this month, while I was in the country, Niccolò came to see me at my country home, where I was handing over some apples to a reseller who had bought them from me. Niccolò told me that Giovanni had spoken to him and that they had agreed that he would talk to Francesco Agata to make him do what he had agreed with Giovanni, but that later he had had second thoughts. He decided not to say anything to Agata, because he knew that he was hare-brained and that it would have been a waste of time to say anything to him. So he had decided that he would rather bear the brunt himself, since he had done so wrong never having told me about the sin that Nencia and Francesco Agata were committing together. He said that now he wanted to do what Giovanni Nelli and I told him to do, and begged me to tell my wife not to say anything to his wife about it.

I told him that in two days he would see Giovanni in Florence and that I thought that we should try to avoid a scandal at all costs.

Then on the 12th of this month Giovanni, Niccolò and I met in Giovanni's shop and agreed that Niccolò would promise in writing to pay Giovanni this coming March one hundred *lire* so that Nencia could get married; and that he should make him his creditor in a bank under the following terms: that when the girl would be given to her husband, Niccolò would cash the dowry that is under Nencia's name in the Monte.[7] I had opened this account for her in May 1471 for 12½ years, spending 4 florins, 3 *lire*, and 12 *soldi*. And when he removed all or part of her dowry from the Monte, Niccolò was obliged to repay me the 4 florins, 3 *lire*, and 12 *soldi*. And since the next morning Giovanni wanted to go to the Mugello, we agreed that in the meantime I would draw up a document containing what is said above, and that they would sign it without any other witnesses so that the affair wouldn't become known. So right there in Niccolò's shop I made three copies in my own hand of the same gist as above, with all of the pledges and agreements. I wrote down the day, that is the 17th of November 1475, and each of them signed all three copies, of which Niccolò kept one, Giovanni the other, and I the other.

I record that yesterday, which was Saturday the 18th of the present month of November 1475, in the evening Giovanni Nelli came to me and told me that that same evening he and Niccolò Macchiavelli had been to see Monna Lisa, the midwife who lives at the Croce a Trebbio in Florence,[8] and that they had arranged to take Lorenza, otherwise known as Nencia di Lazarino, the girl who serves in my house, to her this morning, and that Monna Lisa had promised them that she would keep her until she gives birth. Niccolò had promised to give her five *lire* every month,

---

7. i.e., the *Monte delle Doti* (Dowry Bank), a famous Florentine institution where money was deposited periodically to build up dowries for marriageable young women.

8. A small *piazza* still in existence today, not far from the church of Santa Maria Novella.

and he had given her a florin in advance. So this morning, a little before the 14th hour, Giovanni took Nencia to Monna Lisa's house and my wife let Nencia take all her shifts, handkerchiefs, and other linen. Nencia left my house and went with Giovanni this morning, the 19th of November. Later Giovanni dined with me and told me that he had taken her and left her with Monna Lisa. And for clarity's sake I have recorded it on this 19th day of November.

II.
Niccolò as Pupil and Apprentice; Bernardo Buys Several Books and Has Them Bound

I record that on this 6th day of May 1476, my son Niccolò[9] began to go to Maestro Matteo, the grammar master who lives at the foot of this side of the Santa Trinita bridge, to learn to read the Donatello.[10] And to pay for this teaching I must give him 5 *soldi* per month, plus twenty at Eastertide . . .

I record that on this 8th day of May my son Niccolò brought 5 *soldi* to Maestro Matteo who teaches him, as his salary for this month . . .

I record that on this fifth day of July 1476 I brought to Maestro Niccolò Tedesco, the priest and astrologer, twelve *quinterni*[11] of quarto size, on which I had written all of the cities and provinces, islands, and mountains that are mentioned in Livy's *Decades*, with their addenda according to the books of each of the *Decades*

---
9. Then six years old.
10. The *Ars grammatica* of Elio Donato, a canonical, widely used work during the Middle Ages; the diminutive form "Donatello" indicated the abridged edition that was used in schools.
11. A *quinterno* is a gathering of five folios.

in which Livy mentions them. And he wrote them out for me in Latin, for which he declared himself to be content and satisfied. I had purchased the 3 *Decades* in print from the stationer Zanobi, as we had agreed and as I recorded on folio 4 of this same book, and we also agreed that as a reward for my labors he would bind them for me . . .

I record that on 20 March 1476 my son Niccolò began to go to Ser Battista di Filippo da Poppi to learn the Donatello. Ser Battista gives lessons in the church of San Benedetto in the area of San Giovanni . . .

I record that on this 3rd day of November 1477 I purchased from Francesco Bartoli and company, cloth cutters, 5½ *braccia*[12] of reddish-brown dyed wool cloth from Garbo to make a little tunic and cloak for Niccolò. It came to 10 *lire* and 15 *soldi*. I gave them nine *lire* in cash: 15 *soldi* in a Sienese half florin and 6 *lire* and 18 *soldi* in small change. I still owe them 20 *soldi*. Their boy took the cloth to Leonardo the cloth cutter to have it cut, and left it with his son-in-law Girolamo. He promised me that I could have it back next Thursday morning.

Later I gave them the remaining 20 *soldi* . . .

I record that on this 3rd day of January 1479 I put my son Niccolò to board with Piero Maria, the master of arithmetic and bookkeeping, and we agreed that I would pay him for all this teaching as follows: a half florin when Niccolò begins to study the rudiments of arithmetic, and another later on in the teaching.

On the same day I set Totto[13] to learning the alphabet . . . I record that on the 5th day of November 1481 my sons Niccolò and Totto began to study with Maestro Pagolo da Ronciglione, the grammar master. Niccolò is doing the Latin classics, and Totto is learning Donato; I don't yet have an agreement with Maestro Pagolo about the payment.

I record that on this 21st day of June 1486 I gave to Francesco d'Andrea di Bartolomeo, the stationer at San Giorgio in Florence,

---

12. A unit of measurement roughly equal to 60 cm.
13. Another of Bernardo's sons, born in 1475.

a printed version of a reading of the abbot of Sicily[14] on the 4th and 5th Decretals, in folio, as well as the three *Decades* with the epitome of the 140 books of Livy, printed, also in folio. He is going to bind them well for me, with half-leather boards and two clasps each, and I have agreed to give him four *lire* and 5 *soldi* for binding both volumes. I also agreed to sell him some red wine that he tasted for 50 *soldi* per barrel. He took the books away with him, and promised to bring them back within eight days.

On the same day, in the evening after the 24th hour he came with a porter and took away a barrel of red wine for 50 *soldi*, as we had agreed above.

On the 27th of June I gave him Giovanni d'Andrea's gloss on the sixth Decretal[15] to bind; I bought this from Bartolo di Fruosino, a bookseller in the Garbo,[16] and then Francesco d'Andrea took it to bind it along with the *Mercuriali*,[17] for which he promised to come here this evening when he leaves his shop.

On the same day, at the hour of the Ave Maria, Francesco came here, and I gave him Giovanni Andrea's *Mercuriali* to bind, and we agreed that he would bind them together with the *Novellina* in a single volume with half-leather boards and 2 clasps, for 40 *soldi*. I agreed to give him wine at 50 *soldi* per barrel as above.

I record that on the first of July my son Niccolò gave the stationer Francesco d'Andrea, to whom I had given these books to bind, as is recorded in the preceding page, a barrel of red wine for 50 *soldi*.

On the 4th he gave him 20 *soldi* in cash; for Francesco had said

---

14. "Nicolaus de Tudeschis, abbas Siculus, Lectura super quarto et quinto Decretalium," perhaps the edition published in Pavia in 1482. Nicolò de' Tedeschi (1386–1445) was archbishop of Palermo.

15. "Johannes Andreae, Novella super sexto decretalium," probably the edition published in Pavia in 1483. Giovanni d'Andrea (ca. 1270–1348), a canonist born at Mugello near Florence, was well known for his commentaries on the Decretals of Pope Gregory IX.

16. The modern Via della Condotta.

17. "Johannes Andreae aureum comentum super regulis iuris quod nuncupatur mercuriales," probably also from the 1483 edition published in Pavia.

that he couldn't bind the books without 20 *soldi* to buy the leather.

On the 8th of July Niccolò gave Francesco d'Andrea 3 flasks of red wine and a flask of vinegar, which he came to pick up. So he no longer owed him 5 *soldi*. On the same day, Francesco delivered the bound books. One, the Abbot's reading of the sixth Decretals, was well bound, as we had agreed; the other two were poorly bound and didn't live up our agreement. He did this because I was away in the country.

Lorenzo de' Medici

A Brief Account

A brief account, begun this 15th day of March, 1472,[1] of the course of my life and several other important matters worthy of recollection, for the enlightenment and information of those who shall come after, especially our children.

I find in our father Piero's writings that I was born on the first of January 1448,[2] and that our father and mother, Monna Lucrezia di Francesco Tornabuoni, had seven children — four sons and three daughters — of whom four of us, two sons and two daughters, now remain: that is, my brother Giuliano, myself, 24 years of age, and Bianca, wife of Guglielmo de' Pazzi, and Nannina, wife of Bernardo Rucellai.

I find it written that Giovanni d'Averardo, or Giovanni di Bicci de' Medici, our great-grandfather, died on the 20th day of February, 1428,[3] at the fourth hour of the night,[4] without having made a will. He left an estate of 178,221½ florins bearing the seal of the Mint, as appears in a memorandum in the hand of our grandfather Cosimo on folio 7 of a secret book bound in red leather. The aforementioned Giovanni lived 68 years.

---

1. 1473, according to the modern calendar.
2. i.e., 1449.
3. i.e., 1429.
4. Four hours after sunset.

He left behind two sons, to wit Cosimo, our grandfather, then 40 years of age, and his brother Lorenzo, 30 years of age.

In 1430, Lorenzo had a son, Pierfrancesco, who is alive today. Cosimo had a son, Piero, our father, and Giovanni, our uncle.

In September, 1433 our grandfather Cosimo was arrested in the Palazzo Vecchio, under peril of penalty and capital punishment; and on 9 September he was banished and sent into exile in Padua along with his brother Lorenzo, and on the 11th this was confirmed by the Council of the Balia of 1433; on the 16th of December, 1433 he was given permission to stay in any of the lands of the Venetians, but to come no closer to Florence than Padua.

On the 29th of September 1434, he was recalled to Florence by the Council of the Balia, to the great joy of the whole city, and almost the whole of Italy. He subsequently lived in Florence until the end of his days as the leader of the government of our republic.

Lorenzo de' Medici, the brother of our grandfather Cosimo, passed from this life on the 20th of September 1440, at the age of about 46, at Careggi, at the fourth hour of the night, without making a will. His only heir was his son Pierfrancesco; and at his death it was found that he left an estate of 235,137 florins with the stamp of the Mint, as appears on page 13 in Cosimo's secret book; which estate the aforementioned Cosimo managed on behalf of Lorenzo's son Pierfrancesco, as he did for his own sons Piero and Giovanni, until he was of an appropriate age, as appears in great detail in Cosimo's writings, where he carefully kept an account of everything.

In December, 1451, the estate of the aforementioned Pierfrancesco, who had come of age, was separated from ours by an arbitral decision of Messire Marcello Strozzi, Alamanno Salviati, Messire Carlo Marsuppini, Bernardo de' Medici, Amerigo Cavalcanti, and Giovanni Seristori. By this decision, Pierfrancesco was given half of all of our wealth, giving him a great advantage over us, and all the best items. The notary Ser Antonio Pugi drafted the contract for all of this.

At the same time Pierfrancesco was made a third partner in all of our business dealings, from which he has gained much more than we have, since he has had to spend less.

Lorenzo de' Medici

Our uncle Giovanni, mentioned above, died on the first of November, 1463 at our home in Florence, without making a will, because he had no children and was under his father's authority. Nevertheless, his final wishes were entirely carried out. He had had a son named Cosimo by Monna Ginevra degli Alessandri; this son died in November, 1461, at about 9 years of age.

Our grandfather Cosimo, an extremely wise man, died at Careggi on the first of August, 1464, at the age of about 76, very incapacitated by old age and gout; not only were all of us extremely grieved, but the whole city, and even all of Italy, because he was a very famous man, endowed with many unique talents. He was buried in great state, as much as any Florentine citizen in memory, in the church of San Lorenzo. He did not make a will, nor did he want pomp and ceremony at his funeral. Nevertheless, all of the Lords of Italy sent delegations to honor him and condole at his death, and among others His Majesty Louis King of France ordered that he be honored with his flag — which, out of respect for Cosimo's desires, our father did not allow.

Cosimo was declared "Pater Patriae"[5] by public decree; we have the decree and the letter patent in our home.

After Cosimo's death there was great unrest in Florence; we and our father were particularly harassed, because people were envious of us. Our friends, our social standing, and our belongings were all in great danger. The result was the formation of the general assembly of citizens and other innovations in 1466; Messire Agnolo Acciaiuoli, Messire Dietisalvi, Niccolò Soderini, and several others were banished, and a new government was formed.

In the year 1465, on account of the close ties between our grandfather and our father and the house of France, His Majesty King Louis conferred upon us and decorated our coat of arms with three gold lilies on a blue field, which we still bear today, and for which we have a letter patent with the royal seal affixed to it. This was approved and confirmed in the Palazzo Vecchio by nine votes of the Priors.

---

5. Father of the fatherland.

In the year 1467, in July, there came to us Duke Galeazzo of Milan, who was leading an army in Romagna against Bartolomeo Colleoni of Bergamo, who was assailing our State. Duke Galeazzo stayed in our home by his express wish, although the Signory had arranged to receive him in Santa Maria Novella.

In the same year 1467, around February or March, our father Piero purchased Sarzana, the fortress of Sarzanello, and Castelnuovo in Val di Magra from Messire Lodovico and Messire Tommasino da Campofregosi, in spite of the fact that we were in the middle of a war. The payment was made in Siena by our minister and friend Francesco Sassetti, who was at that time one of the officers of the Monte.[6]

I, Lorenzo, took as my wife the daughter of Signor Jacopo Orsino, Madonna Clarice — or rather she was given to me — on the 4th of June, 1469. Up to this day I have had two children with her, a daugher named Lucrezia, and a son named Piero; and she is with child now. Our daughter's godfather is King Ferrando of Naples, by his request. May God preserve them for us a long while, and protect them from every danger. My wife miscarried two other children, who lived long enough to be baptized.

In July 1469, at the request of the most illustrious Duke Galeazzo, I went to Milan to stand godfather at the baptism of his first-born son, called Giovangaleazzo, in the name of our father Piero; I was much honored there, more than anyone else who was there for the occasion, even though there were men much more worthy than I. And to repay our debt we gave the Duchess a gold necklace with a large diamond, which cost about 3,000 ducats. The result of which was that Signor Galeazzo has wanted me to be godfather to all his other children.

Wishing to do as others do, I jousted in the piazza of Santa Croce, with great expense and extravagance; for which I find I spent around 10,000 florins bearing the seal of the Mint. And though I was neither particularly young nor brawny, I was awarded

---

6. The Florentine Public Fund.

the highest honor, a helmet decorated in silver with the god Mars on the crest.

Piero our father passed from this life on the 2nd of December 1469, very much afflicted with gout. He did not make a will, but an inventory was made and we found ourselves with an estate valued at 237,999½ florins, as appears on page 31 of a large green book in my hand, on vellum. He was buried in the church of San Lorenzo, and we are unceasingly working on building his tomb, and that of his brother Giovanni, as worthily as we can, so that we can lay their bones to rest there. May God have mercy on their souls. My father was greatly mourned by the people of Florence, because he was a man of integrity and of perfect goodness; and we received condolences in letters and from delegations from the most powerful lords of Italy, who offered their States to defend us.

Two days after his death, although I was very young, not having reached the age of 21, the leading men of the city and the State came to our home to mourn with us, and to encourage me to take the reins of the city and the State, as my grandfather and father had done. Since these things were ill suited to my age, and of great responsibility and peril, I accepted unwillingly, and only to safeguard our friends and our wealth, because it is difficult to live as a rich man in Florence without the support of the State. Up to this day we have acted with honor and to the satisfaction of the citizens of Florence; I attribute this not to prudence, but to the grace of God and the good management of my forefathers.

I find we have spent a great deal of money from the year 1434 to now. As appears in a little notebook in quarto from the same year 1434, from 1434 to the end of 1471 we spent an incredible sum, no less than 663,775½ florins, between alms, building, and taxes, not counting other expenses. But I do not mean to complain about this, because although many people might think that it would be better to have someting in your purse, I think that it brings honor to our State, and I believe the money was well spent, and I am well content with this.

In September, 1471, I was elected ambassador to Rome for the coronation of Pope Sixtus IV, and I was greatly honored. And I brought back from thence two antique marble heads of Augustus and Agrippa, which Pope Sixtus IV gave to me, and also our chased chalcedony bowl[7] and many other cameos and medals that I purchased at that time.

---

7. The famous *Tazza farnese* from Lorenzo's collection, now in the Museo Nazionale Archeologico, Naples.

Niccolò Machiavelli
Letter to Francesco Vettori

Florence, 10 December, 1513

To the magnificent Florentine orator Francesco Vettori at the home of his patron and benefactor, the Supreme Pontiff.

Magnificent ambassador,

"The grace of God never comes too late." I say this because I thought I had not lost, but rather temporarily fallen from your favor, for you have not written to me for a very long time, and I was in doubt as to the reason. And none of the possible reasons that occurred to me for your having stopped writing to me seemed plausible, except perhaps that someone had written to you that I hadn't been a good guardian of your letters; and I knew that, outside of Filippo and Paolo, I had shown them to no one. I have now received your letter of the 23rd of last month, and I am very happy to see in what an orderly, quiet way you are carrying out your public office. I encourage you to continue in this way, for I know that the man who neglects his own comfort for the comfort of others loses his own and gains nothing in their eyes. And since Fortune will have her way with everything, she should be left to do as she pleases; we should be calm and not quarrel with her, and await the time when she will do something to mortals. Then it will be well for you to endure more toil, watch after things more, and for me to leave the countryside and say: Here I am. Thus, in this letter of mine I can do no more than tell you about my own life, and if you think it worth trading yours for mine, I will be happy to change it.

I am staying in the country; since those last troubles of mine, I haven't been in Florence more than 20 days in all. Until recently, I had been snaring thrushes with my own hands. I would get up before daybreak, spread bird-lime on twigs, and go out with cages tied around me so that I look like Geta when he returned from the harbor laden with Amphitryon's books.[1] I caught at least two and at most six thrushes each day. And thus I went on for the whole month of September. Then this sport, crude and strange as it might be, came to an end; and what my daily life is now I shall tell you. I arise in the morning with the sun and go off into a wood of mine that I'm having cut, where I stay for two hours reviewing the work from the day before, and passing the time with the woodcutters, who always have some some trouble among themselves or with the neighbors. And I could tell you a thousand things that have happened to me concerning this wood with Frosino da Panzano and others who wanted it. Frosino especially sent for several loads of wood, and when it came time to pay he wanted to withhold 10 *lire*, which he said I owed him from four years ago when he beat me at cards at Antonio Guicciardini's house. I started to make the devil of a fuss; I was about to accuse the carter who had come for the wood of theft. At length Giovanni Machiavelli stepped in, and got us to reach an agreement. Battista Guicciardini, Filippo Ginori, Tommaso del Bene, and several other citizens each ordered a load of wood from me when that wind was blowing. I had promised all of them a load of wood; I sent Tommaso a load, only half of which made its way back to Florence, because he, his wife, their maidservant, and his children

---

1. An allusion to the fifteenth-century popular tale of Geta and Birria, which derived from Plautus' comedy *Amphitryo*. The tale has been attributed to Filippo Brunelleschi and Domenico da Prato, among others.

had reduced it to that, like the butcher Gabburra and his assistants do when they pound beef to made it thinner. So when I saw who was gaining in this transaction, I told the others that I had no more wood. They were all angry, especially Battista, who numbers this among the other disasters that have befallen him in Prato.

When I've left the wood, I go to a spring, and thence to an aviary of mine. I have a book, either Dante or Petrarch, or one of the lesser poets such as Tibullus, Ovid, and the like. I read about their amorous passions, I recall my own, and I enjoy thinking about that for a while. Then I walk down the road to the inn, talk with the passersby, ask for the news from their villages, hear various things, and take note of the diverse tastes and fancies that people have. In the meantime, the hour for the midday meal arrives, and with my company I eat the food that this poor countryside and my tiny property provide. After I've eaten, I return to the inn, where I usually find the innkeeper, a butcher, a miller, and two kilnmen, with whom I spend the rest of the day playing cards and dice and acting like a lout. A thousand disputes and infinite quarrels and insults arise; most times we are fighting over a farthing, and they can still hear us shouting as far away as San Casciano. Thus I keep my brain from getting moldy among these base people, and vent myself for Fortune's malevolence to me, content to let her drive me along this path, to see if she might be ashamed of it.

When evening comes, I return home, and go into my study; on the threshold I take off my daily attire, full of dirt and mud, and put on regal, courtly dress. And thus decently dressed I enter the ancient courts of the men of antiquity where, lovingly received by them, I consume that food which is mine alone, and for which I was born. I am not ashamed to speak with them, and ask them the reasons for their actions; and they in their humanity answer me. And for 4 hours I feel no boredom, I forget all my troubles, I do not fear poverty, and death does not frighten me; I identify totally with them. Because Dante says that there can be no knowledge without retaining what one has learned, I have noted down what I have gained from their conversation, and have written a small work, *De principatibus*, in which I delve as far as I can into this subject, discussing what is a principate, what types of principates there are, how they are acquired, and how they are kept, and why they are lost. And if any of my trifles ever pleased you, this shouldn't displease you; it should be welcome to a prince, and especially to a new prince, so I have dedicated it to the Magnificent Giuliano de' Medici.[2] Filippo Casavecchia has seen it; he can tell you in part both about the work and about the conversations I have had with him, although I am still enlarging and polishing it.

Magnificent ambassador, you would like me to leave this life behind and come to enjoy yours with you. I will do so in any case, but what is holding me back at the moment are certain affairs of mine, which should be concluded within 6 weeks. What makes me doubtful is that the Soderini are in Rome, and if I should go there I would be forced to visit them and speak with them. I would worry that when I return to Florence, instead of going straight home I would be taken to the Bargello.[3] For even though this State has strong foundations and great security, it is also a new state, and therefore suspicious; nor are there lacking know-it-alls like Paolo Bertini who would let other people pay the scot and leave the worrying to me. I pray you, relieve me of this fear. In any event, I shall surely come to visit you within the aforementioned time.

I have discussed with Filippo whether or not I should give this opuscule of mine to Giuliano de' Medici; and if I should give it, whether I should take it to Giuliano in person, or send it. If if don't bring it, I fear that Giuliano won't even read it, and that scoundrel Ardinghelli[4] would take credit for the ideas in this latest work of mine. I feel compelled to give it to him, because I'm wearing myself out, and I cannot go on like this for long without

---
2. Giuliano de' Medici (1479–1516) ruled Florence briefly (from 1512 to 1513) after the Medici were restored to power following the republican rule of 1494–1512.

3. The Bargello was the palace of the *podestà*, the highest judicial and military magistrate of an Italian commune or city-state.

4. Piero Ardinghelli was secretary to Pope Leo X.

Niccolo Machiavelli

becoming despised for my poverty, along with the desire I have that the Medici would start to make use of me, even if they only made me roll a stone. For if I didn't win their favor, I would be very unhappy with myself. If my work were read, people would see that I have been neither sleeping nor playing during the fifteen years that I have been studying the art of statecraft, and they should all be glad to make use of a man who has gained so much experience at the expense of others. And my loyalty to the Florentine State should not be doubted, because, having always remained loyal, why should I now learn to become disloyal? A man who has been loyal for 43 years, which is my age, will not change his character. My poverty testifies to my loyalty and honesty.

Therefore I would desire you to write to me what you think of this matter, and I commend myself to you. Be happy.

Niccolò Machiavelli, from Florence